PULP FASCISM

RIGHT-WING THEMES IN COMICS, GRAPHIC NOVELS, & POPULAR LITERATURE

by

JONATHAN BOWDEN

EDITED BY GREG JOHNSON

Counter-Currents Publishing Ltd.
San Francisco
2013

Copyright © 2013 by Counter-Currents Publishing
All rights reserved

Cover design by
Kevin I. Slaughter

Published in the United States by
COUNTER-CURRENTS PUBLISHING LTD.
P.O. Box 22638
San Francisco, CA 94122
USA
http://www.counter-currents.com/

Hardcover ISBN: 978-1-935965-63-3
Paperback ISBN: 978-1-935965-64-0
E-book ISBN: 978-1-935965-65-7

Library of Congress Cataloging-in-Publication Data

Bowden, Jonathan, 1962-2012, author.
Pulp fascism : right-wing themes in comics, graphic novels, & popular literature / by Jonathan Bowden ; edited by Greg Johnson.
1 online resource.
Includes bibliographical references and index.
Description based on print version record and CIP data provided by publisher; resource not viewed.
ISBN 978-1-935965-65-7 (epub) -- ISBN 978-1-935965-63-3 (hardcover : alk. paper)
1. Comic books, strips, etc.--History and criticism. 2. Graphic novels--History and criticism. 3. Pulp literature, American--History and criticism. 4. Fascism in literature. I. Johnson, Greg, 1971- editor. II. Title.

PN6710
741.5'9--dc23

2013009034

Contents

Foreword by Greg Johnson ♦ iii

The Heroic in Mass & Popular Culture
1. Pulp Fascism ♦ 1
2. From the Last Interview ♦ 26

Comics & Graphic Novels
3. The Comic Book as Linear Energy ♦ 32
4. Batman & the Joker ♦ 35
5. *Arkham Asylum*: An Analysis ♦ 38
6. The Incredible Hulk ♦ 45
7. Judge Dredd ♦ 49
8. Blind Cyclops:
The Strange Case of Dr. Fredric Wertham ♦ 52

Robert E. Howard
9. Robert E. Howard & the Heroic ♦ 56
10. Conan the Barbarian ♦ 81
11. "Rogues in the House" ♦ 85
12. *The Hour of the Dragon (Conan the Conqueror)* ♦ 89
13. Solomon Kane ♦ 100

Pulps
14. H. P. Lovecraft: Aryan Mystic ♦ 104
15. Frank Frazetta: The New Arno Breker? ♦ 108
16. Doc Savage & Criminology ♦ 112
17. Criminology, Elitism, Nihilism:
James Hadley Chase's *No Orchids for Miss Blandish* ♦ 115

Dystopia
18. Mechanical Fruit:
The Strange Case of Anthony Burgess'
A Clockwork Orange ♦ 119
19. George Orwell's *Nineteen Eighty-Four* ♦ 123

20. Eugenics or Dysgenics?
Brian Aldiss' *Moreau's Other Island* ♦ 126
21. Francis Pollini's *Night* ♦ 133
22. Sarban's *The Sound of His Horn* ♦ 137

Popular Drama
23. The Real Meaning of Punch & Judy ♦ 140

APPENDIX
Self-Criticism
24. Why I Write ♦ 165
25. *Apocalypse TV* ♦ 167
26. *Al-Qa'eda MOTH* ♦ 172
27. *Kratos & Other Works* ♦ 175
28. *The Fanatical Pursuit of Purity* ♦ 178
29. *A Ballet of Wasps* ♦ 181
30. *Lilith Before Eve* ♦ 185
31. *Goodbye, Homunculus!* ♦ 188
32. *Louisiana Half-Face* ♦ 191

About the Author ♦ 194

Editor's Foreword

Jonathan Bowden was an avowed elitist and aesthetic modernist, yet paradoxically he had a vast knowledge of and great affection for such forms of popular entertainment as comics, graphic novels, pulp magazines and novels, even Punch and Judy shows, which not only appeal to the masses but also offer a refuge for pre- and anti-modern aesthetic tastes and tendencies.

Left-wing elitists like Theodor Adorno denounced such products of the "culture industry" for their reactionary philistinism. But Bowden was a Right-wing elitist, which is the key to his appreciation of popular culture. Bowden was drawn to popular culture because it was rife with Right-wing themes: heroic vitalism, Faustian adventurism, anti-egalitarianism, biological determinism, racial consciousness, biologically based (and traditional) notions of the differences and proper relations of the sexes, etc.

The present volume collects Bowden's principal statements on Right-wing themes in popular culture, drawing primarily upon works he wrote for the Counter-Currents web and print journal *North American New Right*.

Jonathan was an enthusiastic supporter of Counter-Currents, penning 35 original pieces for *North American New Right* between August 2010 and October 2011. Jonathan also sent us previously published pieces to be reprinted. He was always searching for wider audiences and took particular pleasure when two of his pieces that appeared on Counter-Currents were translated into Czech.

In February 2012, just a month before his death, Jonathan gave a speech, "Western Civilization Bites Back," at a Counter-Currents event in California. He also recorded an interview before flying home in which we discussed his interest in popular culture. Excerpts from that interview are reprinted below. The full interview as well as the speech will appear in another volume from Counter-Currents entitled *Western Civilization Bites Back*, which will appear later this year.

The essays and reviews Jonathan wrote for Counter-Currents were generally short, none of them over 3,000 words, some as short as 600. He told me that he would go to a local public library, where he would check out a computer for a specific period of time. He would open his Hotmail account and address an email to me. Then, without books or notes, he would write out his pieces from memory, as if they were timed university exams, and hit the send key.

On June 23, 2011, it occurred to me that a many of Jonathan's essays explored Right-wing themes in popular culture, so I suggested a collection of essays on this theme entitled *Pulp Fascism*. Jonathan replied the next day, "Yes, I like this idea. I will try and provide another five, six, or seven essays to round out the volume along the lines that you suggest."

He went on to write seven more essays, including "Judge Dredd," "The Incredible Hulk," "Conan the Barbarian," "Solomon Kane," "Rogues in the House," "Doc Savage and Criminology," and "*The Hour of the Dragon*," and it was clear that he was just getting started. In October 2011, however, he took a break.

During his time in California, we talked about finishing the project. The only additional essay topic I recall him mentioning was James Bond. Unfortunately, as far as I know, he never resumed work.

After Jonathan's death, the idea of bringing out a book called *Pulp Fascism* never occurred to me. If I had been asked why, I would have said that there was simply not enough completed material. But in December of 2012, Richard Spencer called me about using "Pulp Fascism" as the theme of a special issue of his journal *Radix*. That got me thinking, and in January of 2013, I opened a file, arranged some titles, added up their word counts, and the present book pretty much fell together.

This volume contains 23 pieces directly related to the "Pulp Fascism" theme: 18 essays from the original outline, an excerpt from Jonathan's last interview, transcriptions of three of Jonathan's speeches, and an excerpt from an earlier book provided by Alex Kurtagić.

The Appendix consists of nine pieces of "Self-Criticism":

Editor's Foreword

Jonathan's credo "Why I Write" and eight reviews of his own books written under the pen name John Michael McCloughlin. Since most of his books draw upon popular as well as *avant-garde* literary forms, and all of them are fascistic, I judged this material a good fit.

This is not, of course, the same book that would have appeared if Jonathan had lived, but it is a worthy vehicle for his thoughts nonetheless.

I wish to thank Michael Woodbridge, Jonathan's literary executor, for his blessing on this project; Michael Polignano, for his help in recording Jonathan's last interview and then in recovering it from a broken flash drive; V. S. and S. F. for transcribing Jonathan's last interview; all the individuals who recorded and made available Jonathan's lectures; John Morgan and Michael J. Brooks for locating a complete recording of Jonathan's lecture on Robert E. Howard, published here as "Robert E. Howard and the Heroic"; John Morgan and V. S. for transcribing the Howard lecture; V. S. for transcribing "Pulp Fascism," the title piece, and "The Real Meaning of Punch and Judy"; Alex Kurtagić for providing "The Comic Book as Linear Energy"; Richard Spencer for inspiring me to revisit and revive this project; Matthew Peters for his careful proofreading; Jef Costello for his photos of Jonathan clowning around with a .44 Magnum; Kevin Slaughter for his always excellent design work; and all the friends and supporters of Counter-Currents without whom this book, and all of the others, would be impossible. I also wish to thank Alex Kurtagić, Ted Sallis, and Richard Spencer for their promotional quotes.

It is with pride tinged with sorrow that I offer this volume in memory of Jonathan's untimely death on March 29, 2012.

Jonathan Bowden said that greatness lies in the mind and in the fist. Nietzsche combined both forms in the image of the warrior poet. For Jonathan, it was the image of the cultured thug. I give you Jonathan Bowden: cultured thug.

Greg Johnson
San Francisco
February 24, 2013

Pulp Fascism*

I would like to talk about something that has always interested me. The title of the talk is "Léon Degrelle and the Real Tintin," but what I really want to talk about is the heroic in mass and in popular culture. It's interesting to note that heroic ideas and ideals have been disprivileged by pacifism, by liberalism tending to the Left, and by feminism, particularly since the social and cultural revolutions of the 1960s. Yet the heroic, as an imprimatur in Western society, has gone down into the depths, into mass popular culture. Often into trashy forms of culture where the critical insight of various intellectuals doesn't particularly gaze upon it.

One of the forms that interests me about the continuation of the heroic in Western life as an idea is the graphic novel, a despised form, particularly in Western Europe outside France and Italy, and outside Japan further east. It's regarded as a form primarily for children and for adolescents.

Almost everyone has come across *Tintin* some time or other. These books/graphic novels/cartoons/comic books have been translated into 50 languages other than the original French. They sold 200 million copies, which is almost scarcely believable. It basically means that a significant proportion of the globe's population has got one of these volumes somewhere.

Now, before he died, Léon Degrelle said that the character of Tintin created by Hergé was based upon his example. Other people rushed to say that this wasn't true and that this was self-publicity by a notorious man and so on and so forth. Probably like all artistic and semi-artistic things, there's an element of truth to it. Because a character like this that's eponymous and archetypal will be a synthesis of all sorts of things. Hergé got out of these dilemmas by saying that it was based upon a

---

* Transcription by V. S. of a lecture entitled "Léon Degrelle and the Real Tintin," delivered at the 21st meeting of the New Right, London, June 13, 2009.

member of his family and so on. That's probably as true as not.

The idea of the masculine and the heroic and the Homeric in modern guise sounds absurd when it's put in tights and appears in a superhero comic and that sort of thing. But the interesting thing is because these forms of culture are so "low," they're off the radar of that which is acceptable, and, therefore, certain values can come back. It's interesting to note that the pulp novels in America in the 1920s and '30s, which preceded the so-called Golden Age of comics in the United States in the '30s and '40s and the Silver Age in the 1960s, dealt with quite illicit themes.

One of the reasons that even today *Tintin* is mildly controversial and regarded as politically incorrect in certain circles is they span much of the 20th century. Everyone who is alive now realizes that there was a social and cultural revolution in the Western world in the 1960s, where almost all the values of the relatively traditional European society, whatever side you fought on in the Second World War, were overturned and reversed in a mass reversion or re-evaluation of values from a New Leftist perspective.

Before 1960, many things which are now legal and so legal that to criticize them has become illegal were themselves illicit and outside of the pedigree and patent of Western law, custom, practice, and social tradition. We've seen a complete reversal of nearly all of the ideals that prevailed then. This is why many items of quite popular culture are illicit.

If one just thinks of a silent film like D. W. Griffith's *Birth of a Nation* in 1915. There was a prize awarded by the American Motion Picture Academy up until about 1994 in Griffith's name. For those who don't know, the second part of *Birth of a Nation* is neo-Confederate in orientation and depicts the Ku Klux Klan as heroic. Heroic! The Ku Klux Klan regarded as the hero, saving the white South from perdition, from the carpetbaggers, some of whom bear an extraordinary resemblance to the present President of the United States of America. Of course, they were called carpetbaggers because they were mulatto politicians who arrived in the South primarily from the North with certain Abolitionist sponsorship, and they arrived with everything they owned in a carpet bag to take over. And that's why they were called that.

That film, which you can get in any DVD store and buy off Amazon for ten pounds or so, is extraordinarily notorious, but in actual fact, in terms of its iconography, it's a heroic, dualist film where there's a force of darkness and a force of light. There's a masculine individual. There are people who believe that they'll sort out problems with a gun. The Bible, in an ultra-Protestant way, is their text. It's what they base metaphysical objectivism and absolute value upon, and that film is perceived retrospectively as an extreme white Right-wing film, although Griffith himself is later to do a film called *Intolerance* and actually, like a lot of film makers, had quite a diverse range of views irrespective of his own Southern and Texan background.

The thing one has to remember is that the methodology of the heroic can survive even if people fight against various forces in Western life. One of the great tricks of the heroic in the last 40 to 50 years is the heroic films involving icons like Clint Eastwood, for example, as a successor to this sort of archetype of John Wayne and the sort of Western stylized masculinity that he represented. Eastwood often plays individualistic, survivalist, and authoritarian figures—Right-wing existentialist figures. But they're always at war with bureaucracies and values that are perceived as conservative. One of the tricks, which has occurred since the 1960s, is to reorient the nature of the heroic so that the eternal radical Right within a society such as the United States or elsewhere is the enemy *per se*.

There's a comic strip in the United States called *Captain America* which began in the 1940s. Captain America is a weedy young man who almost walks with a stick and has arms like branches, and of course a friendly American scientist introduces him to a new secret program where he's injected with some steroids and this sort of thing and immediately becomes this enormous blond hulking superman with blue eyes. Of course, he must dress himself in the American flag so that he can call himself Captain America. So you get the idea! He has a big shield which has the star of the United States on it and has a sidekick who dies in one of the 1940s comics, but of course these figures never die.

They're endlessly brought back. But there's a problem here because the position that Captain America and a lesser Marvel Comics equivalent called Captain Britain and all these other people represent is a little bit suspect in an increasingly liberal society, even then. So, his enemy, his nemesis, his sort of dualist alternative has to be a "Nazi," and of course Captain America has a Nazi enemy who's called the Red Skull.

The Red Skull is a man with a hideous face who, to hide this hideousness, wears a hideous mask over his hideous face as a double take. The mirror cracks, so why not wear a mask? But it's not a mask of beauty. It's a skull that's painted red, and he's called the Red Skull. He always wears green. So, it's red and green. There's always a swastika somewhere in the background and that sort of thing. He's always building robots or cyborgs or new biological sorts of creatures to take over the world. Captain America always succeeds in vanquishing him in the last panel. Just in the last panel. The Red Skull's always about to triumph until the fist of Captain America for the American way and the American dream comes in at the end.

This mantle of the heroic whereby Right-wing existentialists like Captain America fight against the extreme Right in accordance with democratic values is one of the interesting tricks that's played with the nature of the heroic. Because the heroic is a dangerous idea. Whether or not Tintin was based on Léon Degrelle, there is of course a fascistic element to the nature of the heroic. Many writers of fantasy and science fiction—which began as a despised genre but is now, because it's so commercially viable, one of the major European book genres—have always known this. Michael Moorcock, amongst others, speaks of the danger of subliminal Rightism in much fantasy writing where you can slip into an unknowing, uncritical ultra-Right and uncritical attitude towards the masculine, towards the heroic, towards the vanquishing of forces you don't like, towards self-transcendence, for example.

There's a well-known novel called *The Iron Dream*, and this novel is in a sense depicting Hitler's rise to power and everything that occurred in the war that resulted thereafter as a science fiction discourse, as a sort of semiotic by a mad creator.

This book was actually banned in Germany because although it's an extreme satire, which is technically very anti-fascistic, it can be read in a literal-minded way with the satire semi-detached. This novel by Norman Spinrad was banned for about 20 to 30 years in West Germany as it then was. Because fantasy enables certain people to have an irony bypass.

Although comics are quite humorous, particularly to adults, children and adolescents read them, scan them, because they sort of just look at the images and take in the balloons as they go across, because these are films on paper. They essentially just scan them in an uncritical way. If you ever look at a child, particularly a child that's got very little interest in formal literature of a sort that's taught in many European and American schools, they sit absorbed before comics. They're absolutely enthralled by the nature of them, by the absolute villainy of the transgressor, by the total heroicism and absence of irony and sarcasm of the heroic figure with a scantily clad maiden on the front that the hero always addresses himself to but usually in a dismissive way because he's got heroic things to accomplish. She's always on his arm or on his leg or being dragged down.

Indeed, the pulp depiction of women, which, of course, is deeply politically incorrect and vampish, is a sort of great amusement in these genres. If you ever look at comics like *Conan the Barbarian* or *Iron Man* or *The Incredible Hulk* and these sorts of things, the hero will always be there in the middle! Never to the side. Always in the middle foursquare facing the future. The villain will always be off to one side, often on the left; the side of villainy, the side of the sinister, that which wants to drag down and destroy.

As the Hulk is about to hit the Leader, who is his nemesis, or Captain America is about to hit the Red Skull, who is his nemesis, or Batman is about to hit the psychiatric clown called the Joker, who is his nemesis, there's always a scantily clad woman who's around his leg on the front cover looking up in a pleading sort of way as the fist is back here. It's quite clear that these are archetypal male attitudes of amusement and play which, of course, have their danger to many of the assumptions that took over in the 1960s and '70s.

It's interesting to notice that in the 1930s quite a lot of popular culture expressed openly vigilante notions about crime. There was a pulp magazine called *The Shadow* that Orson Welles played on the radio. Orson Welles didn't believe in learning the part. In New York radio Welles, usually the worse for wear for drink and that sort of thing, would steam up to the microphone, he would take the script, and just launch into *The Shadow* straight away.

The Shadow used to torment criminals. Depending on how nasty they were the more he'd torment them. When he used to kill them, or garrote them, or throttle them, or hang them (these pulps were quite violent and unashamedly so) he used to laugh uproariously like a psychopath. And indeed, if you didn't get the message, there would be lines in the book saying "*HA HA HA HA HA!*" for several lines as he actually did people in.

The Shadow is in some ways the prototype for Batman who comes along later. Certain Marxian cultural critics in a discourse called cultural studies have pointed out that Batman is a man who dresses himself up in leathers to torment criminals at night and looks for them when the police, namely the state, the authority in a fictional New York called Gotham City, put a big light in the sky saying "come and torment the criminal class." They put this big bat symbol up in the sky, and he drives out in the Batmobile looking for villains to torment. As most people are aware, comics morphed into more adult forms in the 1980s and '90s and the graphic novel emerged called *Dark Knight* which explored in quite a sadistic and ferocious way Batman's desire to punish criminality in a very extreme way.

There was also a pulp in the 1930s called *Doc Savage*. Most people are vaguely aware of these things because Hollywood films have been made on and off about all these characters. Doc Savage was an enormous blond who was 7 feet tall. He was bronzed with the sun and covered in rippling muscles. Indeed, to accentuate his musculature he wore steel bands around his wrists and ankles. He was a scientific genius, a poetic genius, and a musical genius. In fact, there was nothing that he wasn't a genius at. He was totally uninterested in women. He also had a research institute that operated on the brains of criminals in order to reform them. This is quite extraordinary and deeply politically incorrect! He would not only defeat the villain but at the end of the story he would drag them off to this hospital/institute for them to be operated on so that they could be redeemed for the nature of society. In other words, he was a eugenicist!

Of course, those sorts of ideas in the 1930s were quite culturally acceptable because we are bridging different cultural perceptions even at the level of mass entertainment within the Western world. That which is regarded, even by the time *A Clockwork Orange* was made by Kubrick from Burgess' novel in the 1970s, as appalling, 40 years before was regarded as quite acceptable. So, the shifting sands of what is permissible, who can enact it, and how they are seen is part and parcel of how Western people define themselves.

Don't forget, 40% of the people in Western societies don't own a book. Therefore, these popular, mass forms which in one way are intellectually trivial are in some respects how they perceive reality.

Comics, like films, have been heavily censored. In the United States in the 1950s, there was an enormous campaign against various sorts of quasi-adult comics that were very gory and were called horror comics and were produced by a very obscure forum called Entertainment Comics (EC). And there was a surrogate for the Un-American Activities Committee in the U.S. Senate looking at un-American comics that are getting at our kids, and they had a large purge of these comics. Indeed, mountains of them were burnt. Indeed, enormous sort of semi-book burnings occurred. Pyramids of comics as big as this room would be burnt by U.S. and federal marshals on judges' orders because they contained material that the young shouldn't be looking at.

The material they shouldn't be looking at was grotesque, gory, beyond Roald Dahl sort of explicit material which, of course, children love. They adore all that sort of thing because it's exciting, because it's imaginative, because it's brutal, because it takes you out of the space of normalcy, and that's why the young with their instincts and their passion and glory love this sort of completely unmediated amoral fare. That's why there's always been this tension between what their parents would like them to like and what many, particularly late childish boys and adolescents, really want to devour. I remember Evelyn Waugh was once asked, "What was your favorite book when you were growing up?" And just like a flash he said, "*Captain Blood!*" *Captain Blood!* Imagine any silent pirate film from the 1920s and early '30s.

Now, the heroic in Western society takes many forms. When I grew up, there were these tiny little comics in A5 format. Everyone must have seen them. Certainly any boys from the 1960s and '70s. They were called *Battle*. *Battle* and *Commando* and *War* comics, and these sorts of thing. They were done by D. C. Thomson, which is the biggest comics manufacturer in Britain, up in Dundee. These comics were very unusual because they allowed extremely racialist and nationalist attitudes, but the enemies were always Germans and they were always Japanese.

Indeed, long after the passing of the Race Act in the late 1960s and its follow-up which was more codified and definitive and legally binding in the 1970s, statements about Germans and Japanese could be made in these sorts of comics, which were not just illicit but illegal. You know what I mean, the Green Berets, the commandos, would give it to "Jerry" in a sort of arcane British way and were allowed to. This was *permitted*, even this liberal transgression, because the enemy was of such a sort.

But, of course, what's being celebrated is British *fury* and ferocity and the nature of British warriors and the Irish Guards not taking prisoners and this sort of thing. This is what's being celebrated in these sorts of comics. It's noticeable that D. C. Thomson — who has no connection to the DC group in the United States, by the way — toned down this element in the comics as they went along. Only *Commando* survives, but they still produce four of them a month.

In the 1970s, Thomson, who also did *The Beano* and utterly childish material for children for about five and six as well as part of the great spectrum of their group, decided on some riskier, more transgressive, more punkish, more adult material. So, they created a comic called *Attack*. *Attack!* It's this large shark that used to come and devour people. It was quite good. The editor would disapprove of someone, and they would be eaten by the shark. There were the marvelous balloons they have in comics, something like, "This shark is amoral. It eats." And there would be a human leg sticking out of the mouth of the shark. Some individual the editor disapproved of was going down the gullet.

Now, *Attack* was attacked in Parliament. A Labour MP got up and said he didn't like *Attack*. It was rather dubious. It was tending in all sorts of unwholesome directions. And *Attack* had a story that did outrage a lot of people in the middle 1970s, because there was a story in *Attack* where a German officer from the Second World War was treated sympathetically. Because it was transgressive, you see. What's going to get angry Methodists writing to their local paper? A comic that treats some *Wehrmacht* officer in a sympathetic light. So, there was a real ruckus under Wilson's government in about '75 about this, and so they removed that.

Various writers like Pat Mills and John Wagner were told to come up with something else. So, they came up with the comic that became *Judge Dredd*. *Judge Dredd* is a very interesting comic in various ways because all sorts of Left-wing people don't like *Judge Dredd* at all, even as a satire. If there are people who don't know this, Dredd drives around in a sort of motorcycle helmet with a slab-sided face which is just human meat really, and he's an ultra-American. It's set in a dystopian future where New York is extended to such a degree that it covers about a quarter of the landmass of the United States. You just live in a city, in a burg, and you go and you go and you go. There's total collapse. There's no law and order, and there's complete unemployment, and everyone's bored out of their mind.

The comic is based on the interesting notion that crime is partly triggered by boredom and a sort of wantonness in the masses. Therefore, in order to keep any sort of order, the police and the judiciary have combined into one figure called a Judge. So, the jury, the trial, the police investigation, and the investigative and forensic elements are all combined in the figure of the Judge. So, if Judge Dredd is driving along the street and he sees some youths of indeterminate ethnicity breaking into a store he says, "Halt, citizens! This is the law! I am the law! Obey me! Obey the law!" And if they don't, he shoots them dead, because the trial's syncopated into about 20 seconds. He's given them the warning. That's why he's called Judge Dredd, you see. D-R-E-D-D. He just kills automatically those who transgress.

There's great early comic strips where he roars around on this bike that has this sort of skull-like front, and he appears, and there's a chap parking his car and he says, "Citizen! Traffic violation! Nine years!" and roars off somewhere else. Somebody's thieving or this sort of thing, and he gets them and bangs their head into the street. There's no question of a commission afterwards. "Twelve years in the Cube!" which is an isolation cell. It's got its own slang, because comics, of course, create their own world which children and adolescents love, so you can totally escape into a world that's got a semi-alternative reality of its own that's closed to outsiders. If some adult picks it up and looks at it he says, "What is this about?" Because it's designed to exclude you in a way.

Dredd has numerous adventures in other dimensions and so on, but Dredd never changes, never becomes more complicated, remains the same. He has no friends. "I have no need of human attachments," he once says in a slightly marvelous line. He has a robot for company who provides most of his meals and needs and that sort of thing. For the rest, he's engaged in purposeful and pitiless implementation of law and order. One of his famous phrases was when somebody asked him what is happiness, and he says in one of those bubbles, "Happiness is law and order." Pleasure is obeying the law. And there are various people groveling in chains in front of him or something.

Now, there have been worried Left-wing catcalls, although it's a satire, and it's quite clearly meant to be one. For example, very old people, because people in this fantasy world live so long that they want to die at the end, and they go to be euthanized. So, they all queue up for euthanasia. There's one story where somebody blows up the people waiting for euthanasia to quicken the thing, but also to protest against it. And

Judge Dredd says, "Killing euthanized is terrorism!" War on terror, where have we heard that before? Don't forget, these are people that want to die. But Dredd says, "They're being finished off too early. You've got to wait, citizen!" Wait to be killed later by the syringe that's coming. And then people are reprocessed as medicines, because everything can be used. It's a utilitarian society. Therefore, everything is used from birth to death, because the state arranges everything for you, even though socialism is condemned completely.

There's another bloc—it's based on the Cold War idea—there's a Soviet bloc off on the other side of the world that is identical to the West, but ideologically they're at war with each other, even though they're absolutely interchangeable with each other. But the Western metaphysic is completely free market, completely capitalist, but in actual fact no one works, and everyone's a slave to an authoritarian state.

There's also an interesting parallel with more advanced forms of literature here. *A Clockwork Orange*: many people think it's about Western youth rebellion and gangs of the Rockers and Mods that emerged in the 1960s at the time Burgess wrote his in many ways linguistically overextended work. In actual fact, Anthony Burgess wrote *A Clockwork Orange* after a visit to the Soviet Union where he was amazed to find that, unlike the totalitarian control of the masses which he expected at every moment, there was quite a degree of chaos, particularly amongst the *Lumpenproletariat* in the Soviet Union.

George Orwell in *Nineteen Eighty-Four* has an interesting idea, and that is that the proles are so beneath ideology, right at the bottom of society, the bottom 3% not even the bottom 10%, that they can be left to their own devices. They can be left to take drugs. They can be left to drink to excess. They can be left to destroy themselves. Orwell says "the future is the proles" at one point. Remember when Winston Smith looks out across the tenements and sees the enormous washerwoman putting some sheets on a line? And she sings about her lost love, "Oh, he was a helpless fancy . . ." and all this. And Winston looks out on her across the back yards and lots and says, "If there's a future, it lies with the proles!" And then he thinks to himself, "But looking at them, he had to wonder."

The party degrades the proletariat to such a degree that it ceases to be concerned about their amusements because they're beneath the level of ideology and therefore you don't need to control them. The people you control are the Outer Party, those who can think, those who wear the blue boiler suits, not the black ones from the Inner Party.

This interconnection between mass popular culture, often of a very trivial sort, and elitist culture, whereby philosophically the same ideas are expressed, is actually interesting. You sometimes get these lightning flashes that occur between absolutely "trash culture," if you like, and quite advanced forms of culture like *A Clockwork Orange*, like *Darkness at Noon*, like *Nineteen Eighty-Four*, like *The Iron Heel*, like *The Iron Dream*. And these sorts of extraordinary dystopian and catatopian novels, which are in some respects the high political literature (as literature, literature *qua* literature) of the 20th century.

Now, one of the reasons for the intellectual independence of elements in some comics is because no one's concerned about it except when the baleful eye of censorship falls upon them. A particular American academic wrote a book in the early 1950s called *Seduction of the Innocent* which is about how children were being *depraved* by these comics which were giving them violent and racialist and elitist and masculinist stereotypes, which shouldn't be allowed.

Of course, a vogue for Left-wing comics grew up in the 1970s because culture in the United States, particularly men's culture, is racially segregated in a way which is never admitted. African-Americans have always had their own versions of these things. There are Black American comics. Marvel did two called *The Black Panther*, and the Black Panther only ever preys on villains who are Black.

There's another one called *Power Man* who's in prison loaded down with chains, and a white scientist, who might be Jewish, experiments on him. He's called Luke Cage, and he's experimented on so he becomes a behemoth. A titan of max strength he's called, and he bats down the wall and takes all sorts of people on. And yet, of course, all of the villains he takes on [are black], much like the *Shaft* films—which are very much like the James Bond films, which are very similar. All of this material is segregated. It occurs within its own zone.

But you notice the same heroic archetypes return. Yet again there's a villain in the corner, usually on the left side; Luke Cage has an enormous fist; there's a sort of half-caste beauty on his leg looking up, staring at him. This sort of thing. It's the same main methodology. It's the same thing coming around again.

Although there have been attempts at the Left-wing comic, it's actually quite difficult to draw upon with any effect. Because, in a way you can criticize comics that are metapolitically Right-wing, but to create a Left-wing one is actually slightly difficult. The way you get around it is to have a comic that's subliminally Rightist and have the villain who's the extreme Right. There are two American comics called *Sgt. Fury* and *Sgt. Rock*, and another one's called *Our Army at War. Sgt. Rock*, you know, and this sort of thing. And you know who the villain is because they're all set in the Second World War.

The attitude towards Communism in comics is very complicated. Nuclear destruction was thought too controversial. When formal censorship of comics began in America in the 1950s something called the Approved Comics Code Authority, very like the British Board of Film Classification, emerged. They would have a seal on the front of a comic. Like American films in the 1930s, men and women could kiss but only in certain panels and only for a certain duration on the page as the child or adolescent looked at it, and it had to be—it was understood so explicitly it didn't even need to be mentioned, that *of course* it didn't even need to be mentioned—totally heterosexual. Similarly, violence had to be kept to a minimum, but a certain allowed element of cruelty was permitted if the villain was on the receiving end of it.

Also, the comics had to be radically dualist. There has to be a force for light and a force for darkness. There has to be Spiderman and his nemesis who's Dr. Octopus who has eight arms. But certain complications can be allowed, and as comics grow, if you like, non-dualist characters emerge.

There's a character in *The Fantastic Four* called Dr. Doom

who's a tragic figure with a ruined face, who is shunned by man, who wants to revenge himself on society because he's shut out, who ends as the ruler of a tiny little made-up European country which he rules with an iron hand, and he does have hands of iron. So he rules his little Latvia substitute with an iron hand. But he's an outsider, you see, because in the comic he's a gypsy, a sort of white Roma. But he gets his own back through dreams of power.

There are these marvelous lines in comics which when you ventilate them become absurd. But on the page, if you're sucked into the world, particularly as an adolescent boy, they live and thrive for you. Doom says to Reed Richards, who's his nemesis on the other side, "I am Doom! I will take the world!" Because the way the hero gets back at the villain is to escape, because they're usually tied up somewhere with a heroine looking on expectantly. The hero is tied up, but because the villain talks so much about what they're going to do and the cruelty and appalling suffering they're going to inflict all the time the hero is getting free. Because you have to create a lacuna, a space for the hero to escape so that he can drag the villain off to the asylum or to the gibbet or to the prison at the end. Do you remember that line from *Lear* on the heath? "I shall do such things, but what they are I know not! But they will be the terror of the earth!" All these villains repeat that sort of line in the course of their discourse, because in a sense they have to provide the opening or the space for the hero to emerge.

One of the icons of American cinema in the 20th century was John Wayne. John Wayne was once interviewed about his political views by, of all things, *Playboy* magazine. This is the sort of level of culture we're dealing with. They said, "What are your political views?" and Wayne said, "Well, I'm a white supremacist." And there was utter silence when he said this! He was a member of the John Birch Society at the time. Whether or not he gave money to the Klan, no one really knows.

There's always been a dissident strand in Hollywood, going back to Errol Flynn and before, of people who, if you like, started, even at the level of fantasy, living out some of these heroic parts in their own lives. Wayne quite clearly blurred the distinction between fantasy on the film set and in real life on many occasions. There are many famous incidents of Wayne, when robberies were going on, rushing out of hotels with guns in hand saying, "Stick 'em up!" He was always playing that part, because every part's John Wayne isn't it, slightly differently? Except for a few comedy pieces. And he played that part again and again and again.

Don't forget, *The Alamo* is now a politically incorrect film. Very politically incorrect. There's an enormous women's organization in Texas called the Daughters of the Alamo, and they had to change their name because the white supremacist celebration of the Alamo was offensive to Latinos who are, or who will be very shortly, the Texan majority, don't forget. So, the sands are shifting in relation to what is permitted even within popular forms of culture.

When Wayne said he was a supremacist in that way he said, "I have nothing against other people, but we shouldn't hand the country over to them." That's what he said. "We shouldn't hand the country over to them."

And don't forget, I was born in '62. Obama in many of the deep Southern states wouldn't have had the vote then. Now he's President. This is how the West is changing on all fronts and on every front. American whites will certainly be in the minority throughout the federation in 40 or 50 years. Certainly. Indeed, Clinton—the male Clinton, the male of the species—once justified political correctness by saying, "Well, in 50 years we'll be the minority. We'll need political correctness to fight that game."

The creator of Tintin, Hergé, always said that his dreams and his nightmares were in white. But we know that the politically correct games of the future will be whites putting their hands up in the air complaining because somebody's made a remark, complaining because they haven't got a quota, complaining because this form is biased against them, and this sort of thing. They'll be playing the game that minorities in the West play at the moment, because that's all that's left to them. You give them a slice of the ghetto, you predefine the culture (mass, middling, and elite), in the past but not into the future, elements of the culture which are too much reverent of your past don't serve for the future and are therefore dammed off and not permitted. This is what, in a sense, white people face in America and elsewhere.

One of the great mysteries of the United States that has produced an enormous amount of this mass culture, some of which I have been at times rather glibly describing, is why has there never been a mass serious Right-wing movement of the real Right in the United States. The whole history of the 20th century and before would be different if that had occurred. Just think of it. Not some sort of trivial group, but a genuine group.

Don't forget, the real position of the American ultras is isolationism. They don't want to go out into the rest of the world and impose American neo-colonialism on everyone else. They're the descendants of people who left the European dominion in order to create a new world. Hence, the paradox that the further Right you go in the United States, the more, not pacifist, but non-interventionist you become.

Before the Confederacy, there was a movement called the Know-Nothings, and this is often why very Right-wing people in the United States are described as Know-Nothings. Because when you're asked about slavery, which of course is a very loaded and partial question, you said, "Well, I don't know anything about it." And that was a deliberate tactic to avoid being sucked in to an abolitionist agenda or a way of speaking that was biased in the political correctness of its own era.

But it is remarkable that although the Confederacy didn't have the strength to win, if they had won the history of the whole world would be different. The 20th century would have never taken the course that it did.

One of the interesting things about the American psyche, of course, is that many unfortunate incidents—the war that we fought with the United States in 1812, for example—have been completely elided from history. It's gone! It's gone! We almost went to war with them in 1896 over Venezuela. That still has slightly interesting intonations even now a century or more on when Joseph Chamberlain was Colonial Secretary. This is again elided rather like the Suez incident 1956. There are certain incidents that are played up. And there are anniversaries that are every day on the television, and that you can't escape from. But there are other anniversaries and other events which have been completely airbrushed from the spectrum and from the historical continuum as if they never occurred.

One episode is the extraordinarily bad treatment of prisoners of war by Americans going way, way back. The Confederates and the Unionists treated each other that way in the Civil War, but the Mexicans certainly got the boot in the 1840s, as did the Spanish-Cubans at the turn of the 20th century. Americans beat up every German on principle, including members of Adenauer's future cabinet when they occupied part of Germany. They just regard that as *de rigueur*. This frontier element that is there—crude and virile and ferocious, not always wrong, but ultimately fighting in ways which are not in the West's interests, certainly for much of the 20th century, just gone--is part and parcel of the heroic American sense of themselves.

Where do all of these archetypes ultimately come from? That American popular culture which has gone universal, because the deal is that what America thinks today, the world thinks tomorrow. When we allegedly ruled the world, or part of it, in the 19th century, Gladstone once stood in Manchester in the Free Trade Hall and said, "What Manchester thinks today, the world thinks tomorrow." But now it's what's on MTV or CNN today, that the world would like to think is the ruling discourse of tomorrow.

American self-conceptuality is, to my mind, deeply, deeply Protestant in every sense. Even at the lowest level of their popular culture the idea of the heroic man, often a dissident police officer or a rancher or a hero of certain supernatural powers and so forth, but a man alone, a man outside the system, a man who's anti-Establishment, but he fights for order, a man who believes that everything's settled with a weapon (which is why they always carry large numbers of weapons, these sort of survivalist type heroes). All of these heroes, the ones created by Robert E. Howard, the ones such as Doc Savage and Justice Inc., the Shadow, and all of the superheroes like Batman.

Superman is interesting. Superman is Nietzschean ideas reduced to a thousand levels of sub-intellectuality, isn't it? That's what's going on. He has a girlfriend who never ages called Lois Lane, who looks 22 now even though she's about 88 in the trajectory of the script. There's a villain who's bald called Lex Luthor who's always there, always the nemesis, always plotting. Luthor's reinvented later in the strip as a politician who takes over the city. Superman's clean and wholesome, you see, whereas the villain becomes a politician. You can see the sort of rhetoric.

Luthor and Superman in the stories are outsiders. They're both extraterrestrials. Luthor, however, has anti-humanist values, which means he's "evil," whereas Superman, who's partly human, has "humanist" values. Luthor comes up with amazing things, particularly in the 1930s comics, which are quite interesting, particularly given the ethnicity of the people who created *Superman*. Now, about half of American comics are very similar to the film industry, and a similar ethnicity is in the film industry as in the comics industry. Part of the notions of what is right and what is wrong, what is American and what is not, is defined by that particular grid.

Luthor's an anti-humanite. Luthor always has these thuggish villains who have several teeth missing and are sort of Lombrosian, and they're ugly, have broken noses and slanted hats. This is the 1930s. And Luthor says, "I'm sick of the human. We've got to transcend the human." They don't have words like "transcend" in comics. They say, "go beyond" or something, you know. "We've got to go beyond the human. Humans have got to go! I've got to replace them with a new species." And one of his thugs will say, "Way to go, Luthor! This is what we want!" If you notice, you have a comic called *Superman*, but Superman has liberal values and fights for democracy and the American way, and Luthor, although no one ever says he's "fascistic," is harsh, is elitist, is inegalitarian.

You know that the villains have a tendency to punish their own men? You remember Blofeld in the Bond films? One of his own minions will fail him, and he'll sit in a chair, and you know what's going to happen. A hand strokes the cat with the diamonds around its neck. The villain likes cats, and the cat's eyes stare on. The finger quivers over the button. And Blofeld, or Luthor, or Dr. Doom, or the Red Skull, or the Joker, or whoever it is, because it's the same force really, says, "You failed me. There is only one punishment in this organization . . ." Click! The button goes, and there's an explosion, the bloke screams, goes down in the chair.

There's a great scene in *Thunderball* at the beginning where the chair comes up again. It's empty and steaming, and all the other cronies are readjusting their ties. Blofeld's sat there, and the camera always pans to his hands, the hands of power. You know, the hands of death, the hands of Zeus, the hands of Henry VIII. The closet would meet, and they'd all be disarmed by guards, but he would have a double-headed axe down by the chair.

It's said, by American propaganda, that Saddam Hussein once shot his Minister of Health during a Revolutionary Command Council meeting, and the same script had to be continued in the meeting by the Deputy Minister of Health. Just think of how the Deputy Minister felt! Let's hope he wasn't wearing gray flannels, because they might have been brown by the end of the cabinet session.

This idea of dualism, moral dualism — ultimately a deeply Christian idea in many ways as well as a Zoroastrian idea — is cardinal for the morality of these comics and the popular films and TV serials and all the internet spin-offs and all of these computer games.

Because even when the hero is a woman like Lara Croft and so on, it's the same methodology coming round and round again. Because adolescent boys want to look at somebody who looks like Lara Croft as she runs around with guns in both hands with virtually nothing on. That's the sort of dissident archetype in these American pulps going back a long way. It's just the feminization of heroic masculinity actually, which is what these sort of Valkyries are in popular terms.

Now, the dualist idea is that there's a force for evil and a force for good, and we know who they are: they are the ones out there! In *The Incredible Hulk*, the Hulk is green because he's been affected by gamma rays. The Hulk alternates with a brilliant scientist, but when he's in his monstrous incarnation—because of course it's a simplification of Dr. Jekyll and Mr. Hyde in Robert Louis Stevenson's myth—the Hulk, particularly early on in the comics, is incredibly stupid. If he saw this table in front of him he'd say, "Table. Don't like table." And he'd smash it, because Hulk smashes. That's what he does! He smashes!

The villain in *The Hulk* is called the Leader. The Leader is the villain. The Leader is all brain. Indeed, the Leader has such a long head that he's almost in danger of falling over because of the size of his brain. So, like children have to wear a steel brace on their teeth, the Leader wears a steel brace on his head because he's "too bright." Notice the Leader is a slightly proto-fascistic, Right-wing, elitist figure, isn't he? The man who wants to dominate through his mind—is counterposed by just brute force: the Hulk!

This idea that there's a force for good and a force for evil, and the one always supplants the other, but the one can never defeat the other, because the Leader in *The Incredible Hulk*, the Owl in *Daredevil*, the Joker in *Batman*, Dr. Doom in *The Fantastic Four*, Dr. Octopus and the Green Goblin (another green one) in *Spiderman* . . . they're never destroyed. If one of them is destroyed, their son finds their mask in a trunk and puts it on and knows that he wants to dominate the world! And comes back again. They can never be destroyed because they're archetypes.

The comics hint at a sort of pagan non-dualism partly because they insist upon this good and evil trajectory so much. That's in some ways when they become quite morally complicated and quite dangerous.

In Greek tragedy, a moral system exists, and it's preordained that you have a fate partly in your own hands even though it's decided by the gods. In the *Oresteia* by Aeschylus, you have a tragedy in a family (cannibalism, destruction, self-devouring) which is revenged and passed through into future generations. So that the Greek fleet can get to Troy, a girl is sacrificed. Clytemnestra avenges herself as a Medusa, as a gorgon against her husband who has killed her own daughter. Then, of course, there's a cycle of revenge and pity and the absence of pity when the son, Orestes, who identifies with the father, comes back.

In this type of culture, and obviously a much higher level conceptually, it's noticeable that the good characters and the evil characters align, are differentiated, merge, replace one another, and separate over the three plays in that particular trilogy.

If you look at real life and you consider any conflict between men, Northern Ireland in the 1970s (we're British here and many people here are British nationalists). But if you notice the IRA guerrilla/terrorist/paramilitary, the Loyalist guerrilla/terrorist/paramilitary . . . One of my grandfathers was in the Ulster Volunteer Force at the beginning of the 20th century, but I went to a Catholic school.

Nietzsche has a concept called perspectivism whereby certain sides choose you in life, certain things are prior ordained. When the U.S. Marine fights the Islamist radical in Fallujah, the iconography of an American comic begins to collapse, because which is the good one and which is the evil one? The average Middle American as he sat reading *Captain America* zapping the channels with a sort of 30-second attention span thinks that the Marine is the good one.

But at the same time, the Marine isn't an incarnation of evil. He's a man fighting for what he's been told to fight for. He's a warrior. There are flies in his eyes. He's covered in sweat. He's gonna kill someone who opposes him. But the radical on the other side is the same, and he sees that he's fighting for his people and the destiny of his faith. And when warriors fight each other, often there's little hatred left afterwards, because it's expended in the extraordinary ferocity of the moment.

This is when this type of mass culture, amusing and interesting and entertaining though it is, begins to fall away. Because whenever we've gone to war, and we've gone to war quite a lot over the last 10 to 12 years. Blair's wars: Kosovo. There's the bombing of the Serbs. Milošević is depicted as evil! Remember those slogans in *The Sun*? "Bomb Milošević's bed!" "Bomb his bed!" "Bomb his house!" And this sort of thing. Saddam! "We're gonna string him up!" "The man's a war criminal!" The fact he'd been a client to the West for years didn't seem to come into it. Hanged. Showed extreme bravery in a way, even though if you weren't a Sunni in Iraq, definitely, he wasn't exactly your man.

There's a degree to which the extraordinary demonization of the other works. That's why it's used. The British National Party won two seats in that election but there was a campaign against it for 12 to 15 days before in almost every item of media irrespective of ideological profile saying, "Don't vote for these people!" to get rid of the softer protest votes, and you're only left with the hard core. That's why that type of ideology is used. Maybe humans are hardwired to see absolute malevolence as on the other side, when in actual fact it's just a person who may or may not be fighting against them.

But this type of mass or popular culture retains the instinct of the heroic: to transcend, to fight, to struggle, to not know fear, to if one has fear to overcome it in the moment, to be part of the group but retain individual consciousness within it, to be male, to be biologically defined, to not be frightened of death, whatever religious or spiritual views and values that one incarnates in order to face that. These are, in a crude way, what these forms are suggesting. Morality is often instinctual, as is largely true with humans.

I knew somebody who fought in Korea. When they were captured, the Koreans debated amongst themselves whether they should kill all the prisoners. There were savage disputes between men. This always happens in war.

I remember, as I near the close of this speech, that one of Sir Oswald Mosley's sons wrote a very interesting book both about his father and about his experiences in the Second World War. This is Nicholas Mosley, the novelist and biographer. He was in a parachute regiment, and there are two stories that impinge upon the nature of the heroic that often appears in popular forms and which I'll close with.

One is when he was with his other members. He was with his other parachutists, and they were in a room. There was *The Daily Mirror*, still going, the organ of Left-wing hate which is *The Daily Mirror*, and on the front it said, "Oswald Mosley: The

Most Hated Man in Britain." *The most hated man in Britain*. And a chap looked up from his desk and looked at Mosley who was leading a fighting brigade and said, "Mosley, you're not related to this bastard, are you?" And he said, "I'm one of his sons." And there was total silence in the room. Total silence in the room, and they stared each other out, and the bloke's hands gripped *The Mirror*, and all the other paratroopers were looking at this incident. And after about four minutes it broke, and the other one tore up *The Mirror* and put it in a bin at the back of the desk and said, "Sorry, mate. Didn't mean anything. Really." Mosley said, "Well, that's all right then, old chap." And left.

The other story is very, very interesting. This was they were advancing through France, and the Germans are falling back. And I believe I've told this story before at one of these meetings, but never waste a good story. A senior officer comes down the track and says, "Mosley! Mosley, you're taking too many prisoners. You're taking too many prisoners. It's slowing the advance. Do you understand what I'm saying, Mosley?" And he said, "Sir, yes, I totally understand what you're saying." He says, "Do you *really* understand what I'm saying? You're slowing the advance. Everyone's noticing it. Do something about it. Do you understand?" "Sir!"

And he's off, I guess to another spot of business further down. Mosley turns to his Welsh sergeant-major and says, "What do you think about that? We're taking too many prisoners." Because what the officer has told him in a very English and a very British way is to shoot German soldiers and to shoot German prisoners and to shoot them in ditches. What else does it mean? "You're slowing the advance! You're taking too many prisoners! You're not soft on these people, are you, Mosley? Speed the advance of your column!" That's what he's saying, but it's not written down. It's not given as a formal and codified order. But everyone shoots prisoners in war! It's a fact! When your friend's had his head blown off next to you, you'd want revenge!

I know people who fought in the Falklands. And some of the Argentinian Special Forces and some of the conscripts together used dum-dum bullets. Hits a man, his spine explodes.

So, when certain conscripts were found by British troops they finished them pretty quickly at Goose Green and elsewhere. This will occur! In all wars! Amongst all men! Of all races and of all kinds! Because it's part of the fury that battle involves.

One of my views is that is that we can't as a species, or even as groups, really face the fact that in situations of extremity this is what we're like. And this is why, in some ways, we create for our entertainment these striated forms of heroic culture where there's absolutely good and absolutely malevolent and the two never cross over. When the Joker is dragged off, justice is done and Inspector Gordon rings Batman up (because it is he) and says, "Well done! You've cleansed the city of a menace." All of the villains go to an asylum called Arkham Asylum. They're all taken to an asylum where they gibber insanely and wait for revenge against the nature of society.

I personally think that a great shadow has been cast for 60 years on people who want to manifest the most radical forms of political identity that relate to their own group, their own inheritance, their own nationality, their own civilizational construct in relation to that nationality, the spiritual systems from the past and in the present and into the future that are germane to them and not necessarily to the others, to their own racial and biological configuration. No other tendency of opinion is more demonized in the entire West. No other tendency of opinion is under pressure.

Two things can't be integrated into the Situationist spectacle based upon the right to shop. They're religious fundamentalism and the radical Right, and they're tied together in various ways. It's why the two out-groups in Western society are radical Right-wing militants and Islamists. They're the two groups that are Other, that are totally outside. The way in which they're viewed by *The Mirror* and others is almost the level of a Marvel Comics villain.

I seem to remember a picture from the *Sunday Telegraph* years ago of our second speaker [David Irving], and I'm quite sure that it'd been re-tinted, at least this is my visual memory of it, to appear darker, to appear more sinister. I remember once *GQ* did a photo of me years ago when I was in a group called Revolutionary Conservative. That photo was taken in Parliament Square. You know, the square that has Churchill *and* Mandela in it, that square near our parliament, with Oliver Cromwell over there hiding, Boadicea over there hiding further on. That photo was taken at 12:30, and it was a brighter day than this. But in *GQ* magazine it was darkened to make it look as though it was shot at nine o'clock, and everything was dark, and because it involved so much re-tinting it slightly distorted and reconfigured everything. That's because these people are dark, you see! They're the force from outside! They're that which shouldn't be permitted!

Whereas I believe that the force which is for light and the force which is for darkness (because I'm a pagan) can come together and used creatively and based upon identity and can lead on to new vistas. But that's a rather dangerous notion, and you won't find it in *The Fantastic Four* when Reed Richards and Dr. Doom do battle, and you won't find it in *Spiderman* when Peter Parker and Dr. Octopus (Dr. Otto Octavius) do battle with one another. You won't see it when the Aryan Captain America is taking on his National Socialist nemesis, the Red Skull. You won't see it with the Hulk taking on the Leader. You won't see it in any of these forms. But these forms have a real use, and that is that they build courage.

Nietzsche says at the end of *Zarathustra* that there are two things you need in this life. You need courage and knowledge. That's why Zarathustra has two friends. He has an eagle, which stands for courage, and he has a snake, which stands for knowledge. And if you can combine those things, and synthesize them, you have a new type of man and a new type of future. And Nietzsche chose the great Persian sage as the explicator of his particular truth, because in the past he represented extreme dualism, but in the future Nietzsche wished to portray that he brought those dualities together and combined them as one heroic force.

Thank you very much!

Counter-Currents/*North American New Right*
March 25, 2013

From the Last Interview*

GREG JOHNSON: You are an author as well as a reader of comics and graphic novels.

JONATHAN BOWDEN: Yes, when I was a child and an adolescent. Yes.

GJ: That's a quintessentially popular art form. It's directed primarily to children and young adults, and yet you think that it has a great deal of aesthetic potential. Can you talk a little bit about your sense of that?

JB: Yes, it's an interesting one because that's very much an art for and of the masses. And although I am an elitist, there are moments when you wish to communicate with the majority of people. I suppose the thing that attracted me to them when I was very young was the heroic. The heroic is denied in our culture in all sorts of ways and has been disprivileged. Those forces that animated the great epics and Homer have been forced down to the level of comic books literally. Because the heroic is not seen as a necessary or requisite part of a high culture.

When you have liberal values supervising the novel and the elite play and the elite film, the heroic will go down into the lowest forms of mass culture. And yet really what are comics? They're films on paper, and in certain cultures, like Japan and so on, they're considered to be genuine art forms of quite a high sort. That isn't true in the West, but because they are representational and yet very imaginative. You can communicate with a large number of people instantaneously, and you can also be stereotypical in relation to the heroic which is more dif-

---

* Excerpts from a transcription by V. S. and S. F. of Jonathan Bowden's Last Interview, http://www.counter-currents.com/2013/01/jonathan-bowdens-last-interview-part-2/

ficult with more complicated forms.

There is also a degree to which the art can be actually quite abstract, because it's draughtsmanship *par excellence*, and it's only lines on paper. And if you look at the imaginative input into what is purely a commercial area, there's this odd trade-off between the aesthetic quality and the risible quality in terms of psychological realism and sociological appropriateness.

But that's not what these things are about. They are also a pure form of escape and a pure form of sub-literary escapism, and I quite like art as a sort of escapism because we're all born, we're all going to die, and there needs to be something to fill the gap in between.

GJ: The graphic novel has emerged as a more artistically serious form of comic book, and for a long time I have to admit that I was somewhat dismissive of this. First of all, people were touting Spiegelman's *Maus*, and I thought that this was very tendentious anti-cat propaganda. How is this an improvement on the comic book, and how is this serious as art?

Then I started discovering that movies that I thought were really rather good, like *A History of Violence*, were based on graphic novels, and so I started looking into them. I really am very impressed specifically with the graphic novel *Watchmen*, which I think is as a novel really on the level of some 19th century Romantic novels of the highest order. What do you think of the graphic novel, and what do you think its future is, its potential is?

JB: Well, its potential . . . because they really are films on paper. There's no denying that they are what it says on the tin. Therefore, the commercial pressures aside, their artistic future is limitless because it's as limitless as the capacity to create stories and to visualise them. So, all that will hold them back is the absence of seriousness with which they are viewed by the general, more literate culture. It's probably true that mass culture is more visual than elite culture. Because elite culture tends to be more conceptual and tends to be bound by words.

Now, in these types of graphic novels you have sequential

art with a storyboard that is a film on paper and so you do have the ability to create films very cheaply. In some ways, it's a marvellous medium because it approximates to Wagner's total art form because with the exception of music you've got almost everything combined.

There's always something slightly ridiculous about comics, even the highfalutin ones that we're discussing at the moment, but that's part of their charm. They do have a charm. They do have a kitsch, which is part of their romantic allure. Because the first literature that most children fall in love with actually, long before they come to books, they look at this sort of material. Even if they quickly outgrow it.

GJ: Who do you think are the best graphic novelists and what are the best graphic novels?

JB: There's a *Batman* called *Arkham Asylum* which is by Dave McKean—visually anyway—and which is quite extraordinary. That was done before computers became fashionable. To paint on a computer screen and to print it out is how that sort of art form is now done, but McKean did individual paintings. Each of those panels is an individual painting situated within a larger conspectus.

I suppose Alan Moore. I don't care for Alan Moore's sort of politics particularly, insofar as it's subliminally present in his work, but he would have to be considered as a major talent in the area that he's chosen to concentrate in.

Again, you tend to scan this sort of material. You don't so much read it as you scan it. It's very much like watching film. You absorb it. It's like the windscreen wipers in a car—flick, flick—and then you go to the next page, and you absorb it almost osmotically. You float in this material and then put it down.

In this sense it's probably more powerful than visual art, although visual art can reach parts of the mind that nothing else can, because it's not bounded by narrative, and yet if you bound images by narrative, you have the possibility of reaching very large numbers of people. It's surprising in some ways that graphic novels haven't even been even more successful than they could be, but that's probably because television is in the way and the DVD is in the way. If those forms were less pronounced, probably they'd have an even greater articulacy than they do at the present time.

GJ: You said that the graphic novel is like the Wagnerian total work of art except that it lacks music, which brings to mind the movies that have been made from graphic novels, which of course include music. One of my theses is that the movie really is the thing that most closely approximates Wagner's idea of the complete work of art, because with Wagner you still had the staging necessities of the theatre that sort of constrict your points of view whereas film doesn't have those constrictions and therefore it's more versatile, yet it can incorporate all the other art forms like the complete work of art was supposed to do. Do you think that's a sensible thesis?

JB: Very much so. Yes. Film is the ultimate art form of the 20th century and contains all the other arts within itself. That's why it was important to try and make films. Film is the most frustrating thing to do, however. Because it involves radical collaboration with other people and with other egos, and it's costly, and it's extraordinarily time-consuming to do properly. It involves great technical skill and ingenuity.

However, digital film-making has democratized the film industry even though in the end these films are just cut up and put on YouTube or its equivalent. But you can now make films for very little money. The films that I've made cost £800 pounds each, which is totally ridiculous in relation to what film technology once cost in the past.

But, yes, I've always wanted to make films actually because films are the total way in which you can live a dream which can impact upon other people and also can be seen in a relatively short and sequential period of time. It takes maybe 8, 10, 16, 24 hours to read a book sequentially over a period. An image can be accessed in seconds, that's true. But a film you can put life, death and everything else into a spectacle that lasts for one hour. There is probably nothing like it.

GJ: Ayn Rand had an essay called "Bootleg Romanticism" where she talked about certain forms of popular literature in the 20th century that she thought were a refuge where 19th century Romanticism had fled because it had been purged by naturalism and modernism and the sort of higher letters. She talks about things like spy shows. She talks about *The Man from U.N.C.L.E.*, although she dropped that from the published version of that essay when she put it in her book *The Romantic Manifesto*. She talks about the Bond films. She talks about pulp adventure novels and things like that.

You have a great interest in pulp novels . . .

JB: . . . Raymond Chandler . . .

GJ: You have an interest in pulp and popular fiction. Is that true?

JB: Yes, partly because its crudity is endlessly amusing and also its love of the extreme and its love of the radical situation is compelling.

I'm drawn to extremism. I've always been an extremist. But I'm not drawn to the usual forms of counter-bourgeois extremism that exist on the Left. So, with me, the elitist spine that has to subsist in everything prevents me from going in a Leftwards direction because egalitarianism is a bore. There's nothing more boring than egalitarianism. There's nothing more aesthetically sterile. And that's why the truth is on the Right side of the equation.

As for popular forms: popular forms can be very mass-oriented and degraded, but they can also be endlessly charming and full of life and brio and energy, and in their very crudity they can escape some of the halting steps that the naturalist aesthetic might place upon things. It's the very abnaturalism and non-naturalism of elements of the popular imagination, as perceived artistically in mass culture, that can render the grotesque even more baleful, even more illuminating, even more distressingly actual.

GJ: You like Robert E. Howard. You've done a lot of writing about his *Conan* works and other writings. Again, this is a fellow who created a lot of popular literature, yet you are drawn to it even as an anti-egalitarian elitist.

JB: Yes, that's right. Partly just because of the heroic metaphysic which is itself a form of elitism, as Rand rightly pointed out. Things are never destroyed in culture. They're just displaced, and therefore they find new levels for themselves through which they can articulate what they are or might be. So, naturalistic fiction displaced fantasy fiction, which went down into genres like fantasy and science fiction and the rest of it, and those come up again and become more literary in the hands of somebody like Ballard.

Whereas popular work and elitist work fertilize each other and interrelate. With me things are never either/or but yes/and, and there's a degree to which you can see ramifications of the elite in the popular, and you can see dithyrambic populism in elitism. It's more the treatment and the self-overbecoming which is involved in any creative moment. It's less whether there's something that's popular or whether something is populist or whether something is elitist. Life and history will determine that.

Howard is now regarded in part as a sort of, not as an elite writer, but as a qualified elite writer; certainly as a literary writer, which as pulpster he was never considered to be. Indeed, the triumvirate of the *Weird Tales* three—Lovecraft and Clark Ashton Smith and Robert E. Howard—are now considered to be essentially elitist writers who went slumming.

THE COMIC BOOK AS LINEAR ENERGY*

One of the most interesting and despised areas of popular culture is the "funny book" or comic—although the comic book itself has now become a prized form, with the original frames of *Batman* and *Superman* fetching large prices at Sotheby's and other art dealers. The early comics, such as *Batman* and *Superman*, were staples of DC comics, based in the Rockefeller Plaza. They were adventure stories for boys, though comics were later to split along the styles of gender specification, and boys enjoyed superhero comics, perhaps *War and Battle* as well, while girls tended towards romantic comics dealing, in a crude way, with "human situations," such as *Cindy* magazine. One can almost hear feminist devotees clucking in the background, but gender specification is an inalienable fact, a biological reality.

Nevertheless, Batman and Superman were subtly different from each other, and while Superman was more rugged, more all-American, Batman was darker and had more Gothic potential. Indeed, Batman was a mere mortal, unlike Superman, an expression of the vigilante urge in American society. In accordance with liberal stereotypes, of course, Batman was an individual who liked dressing in sadomasochistic uniforms and "beating the hell out of criminals." He was obviously a man who showed *"fascistic symptoms"*—elements of pathological retribution, based on the murder of his parents, the Waynes. While Batman himself represented a dark, Gothic atmosphere, his villains, who reappeared in issue after issue, were his *alter egos*. Moreover, they appeared to be necessarily *lightweight*; they were villains of humor, charlatans of deviousness, like the Joker, the Riddler, and the Penguin.

The Joker is an interesting figure: a man who always murders his opponents with a smile on his face. This is basically

---

*Excerpted by Alex Kurtagić from a book called *Scum*, written in 1992.

The Comic Book as Linear Energy

because the smile, the broken leer, is unmovable; it was fixed there either by acid or a radioactive explosion, I cannot remember which — but, unlike Doctor Doom, the villain in *The Fantastic Four*, a Marvel comic which came along later, the Joker is not a genuinely tragic figure.

Doctor Doom, on the other hand, is a marvelous character, a man who has been terribly disfigured by a chemical explosion. As a result of this, he locks his face and eventually his whole body away in a suit of armor, later covered with beige cloth. Like *The Phantom of the Opera* in Gaston Leroux's novel, no-one can see his face without being completely incapacitated — one of the reasons why it has never been shown in a comic panel.

In a sense, therefore, comic books represent orgies of violence, ugliness, meaninglessness, and sadomasochistic violence. Indeed, it is not surprising that Marvel Comics later introduced a character called the Punisher, first as a villain in *Spiderman*, and then as a hero or anti-hero in his own strip.

Marvel also brought out a highly sophisticated and degenerate comic called *Deathlok*, which featured a strange freak of science fiction: a half-human robot; a robot which was actually a reanimated and rotting corpse — the corpse of a marine commando, held in a metal casing and with part of its brain replaced by a computer ('puter), with which the cyborg engaged in constant mental jousts.

As can be seen from the above, these comics were an amphitheater of perversion, a cruel tourney, available in any dime house, over which children would pore for hours, much to the consternation of their parents. Not surprisingly, there are periodic attempts (by parents and guardian committees, watchdogs, and so forth) to ban or restrict the circulation of such material, and under threat by a Congressional committee that was concerned about "horror comics," the industry bowed to the inevitable and introduced a voluntary body, the Comics Code Authority.

Of course, the whole purpose of comic books is that they are cruel "jokes," violent forms of juvenilia, which focus and dispel the raw emotions of children. In a sense they are the violent fantasies of children, where no-one is ever hurt and everyone picks themselves up at the end of the day.

Hence, we see the purposeless energy, the violent and contrary lines of force that comic books represent. They are festivals of line, disorientated patterns of force—just look at the *Modesty Blaise* strip by Peter O'Donnell, for instance, and you will realize that they are the *sine qua non* of Right-wing art. They are a festival of linear force—nothingness, despair, redemption, where redemption involves commitment, in the Sartrean sense, nearly always through violent action.

This is the type of act represented by *Rapeman* in the Japanese adult comics known as *manga*, where beautiful and dreamy Oriental women, drawn in outline, are sexually assaulted and murdered by Rapeman. Moreover, such draughtsmanship always accentuates the sexual organs of women, as in the *Vampirella* strip, for example.

The *Vampirella* strip, in particular, dealt with the adventures of a scantily clad Transylvanian countess. In many respects, it was an attempt to corner two markets at once: namely, the market for horror stories, on the one hand, and the market for soft pornography, on the other. Moreover, you can be sure such comics were not licensed by the Comics Code Authority.

Wermod & Wermod
February 2, 2013

BATMAN & THE JOKER

The Brave and the Bold
A Team-up comic featuring Batman and the Joker
DC Comics, No. 111, March 1974

    This comic was published in 1974 by DC comics or National Periodical Publications. It retailed for twenty cents, and I bought it in the United Kingdom for eight new pence. The author was the veteran scripter Bob Haney, and it was drawn by Jim Aparo. None of the other contributors—the inker, colorist, letterer, or editor—is recorded.

    The whole point of looking at this comic is that it dovetails with the review of the film *The Dark Knight* elsewhere on this site.[1] Yet there are important differences—the directness or crudity of the form, its clientele of adolescent boys, and the amount of censorship it was under pulls it in a dissimilar direction.

    There is no room for the Joker, his arch nemesis, to philosophize about Batman falling short as a superman. For the very insistent dualism or absence of moral relativism means that the Joker's actions—not his words—are depicted in a despicable light. But this has an unintentional result, in that it makes Batman less liberal, more ferocious, vengeful, and "fascistic." The center of gravity then shifts, and the police commissioner, Gordon, is forever trying to restrict Gotham's finest, curb him from vigilantism, and keep him on the straight and narrow.

    The story involves the Joker wiping out a totally respectable family who had the temerity to inform on a criminal. He did it as a response to normal society and as a sort of Stirnerite *aporia*—a nihilistic and anti-social act. Batman is outraged and swears an implacable vengeance. He threatens to Gordon that he will kill this sadistic clown once and for all. Gordon sniffs: "We're here to

---

    [1] Trevor Lynch, Review of *The Dark Knight*, Counter-Currents/*North American New Right*, September 27, 2010, http://www.counter-currents.com/2010/09/the-dark-knight/

represent the Law, Batman, no vigilante stuff." To which Batman sneers: "You better find him first if you want to bring him in alive!"

There then occurs several quite complicated somersaults or backflips in the plot—thereby confirming that comics are very close to both film and television, being heavily plot-driven. The Joker allegedly returns to Gotham's morgue in order to mutilate his victims with the rictus leer which is his trademark. Why? Had he forgotten to do so?

Gradually, via an underworld tip-off, Batman tracks the purple-clad and green-haired minstrel to a lonely gravel barge (now disused). Another clue leads to a Turkish steam bath where he pounces upon the Joker as he hunts an underworld killer called Slade. Batman is wounded in the encounter, but survives.

Little by little, it dawns on Commissioner Gordon and Batman that the Joker is innocent, that he's hunting the real slayer, Slade, and that to capture the latter will involve *collaborating with the Joker*. (Note: Is there, no matter how subliminally, a notion of wartime collaboration here? Who knows?)

The Joker and Batman contact each other so as to bring home the ghastly deed to Slade. The Joker taunts and berates Batman throughout—yet there remains this strange attraction, symmetry, and false "completeness" between them. After various shenanigans, involving a chase sequence following the auction of an old gangster's Cadillac, the final element of the drama supervenes.

Throughout all of this, though, Batman has become more and more maniacal. He strong-arms criminals, roughs up a morgue attendant, disobeys police orders, is placed under arrest by Gordon ("see that Batman doesn't leave this room"), and plots openly to murder the Joker.

I believe that a comic like this has to be as either/or . . . or as Manichean as possible, morally speaking. A film can be 18 or X-certificate, and the era of graphic novels "suggested for the mature reader" didn't exist then. All mainstream comics were severely vetted or controlled and subject to a censorship board— just like in early Hollywood. Hence we see the moniker which appeared on the front of such works that read "Approved by the

Comics Code Authority."

Such strictures often led to barely suppressed adolescent fantasies—very much unconstrained in young boys—of violence, energy, revenge, or transgression. But this occurs also, don't forget, at the hands of the hero. In these works the moral *alter ego* of Batman is Gordon, the police chief, not the Joker. The villain must be utterly repulsive and crepuscular . . . yet this opens up the "dangerous" notion of justified revenge on behalf of the illiberal masses. Given their lowness as a form, comics can luxuriate in the "badness" of the hero—even to the point of pitilessness.

For example, the pulp magazine from the '30s, *The Shadow*, that Batman slightly resembles, luxuriated in vigilantism, sadism, punishment of criminals, and revenge by one's fireside. The radio show based on it was the most listened to in America at that time. Orson Welles played the virtual anti-hero.

Anyway, by the comic's conclusion, Batman, Slade, and the Joker are in their rightful places. It is all revealed to have been a plot to assassinate Batman in a disused canal lock. The Joker and Slade are accomplices. They are cold-blooded psychopaths. Batman is their eternal enemy. Yet he turns the tables on them, escapes from underwater, kicks Slade unconscious, and pursues the Joker towards the sports car: the Batmobile. The man who smiles without mirth can't start it and is beaten by the Avenger, but, under the Code, a moral ending must be enforced. All collaboration is spent. Batman overcomes his desire to enact an extra-juridical killing. The Joker will be returned to a state correctional institution for the criminally insane, Arkham Asylum.

Nonetheless, for a brief moment the Joker and Batman were on the same side against Gordon (and Slade), prior to the inevitable reversal. The idea remains notwithstanding that the dramaturgy between these characters can become more complex—if adult psychology and philosophy is added. Finally, such a comic (virtually forgotten now and a third of a century old) exemplifies the *naked fascism of the heroic avenger* up to the penultimate frame.

Counter-Currents/*North American New Right*
November 14, 2010

ARKHAM ASYLUM:
AN ANALYSIS

Arkham Asylum: A Serious House on Serious Earth
Story by Grant Morrison, art by Dave McKean
New York: DC Comics, 1989

Arkham Asylum claims to be among the most "adult" comics ever produced, and, although there are a few other candidates, it does merit this accolade up to a point. It has also inspired numerous spinoffs, including video games. Elsewhere I have written about a Batman and the Joker team-up comic from the mid-seventies, but this was deliberately circumscribed by the Comics Code Authority and lacked a mature sensibility.

Note: By "adult," I am not referring to a predilection for transgression, low-grade, or "edgy" material here. Most of these attempts in popular culture are faintly ludicrous, it has to be said. No. What I am referring to is transgression of the philosophical limitations placed on such narratives by an insistent Dualism. This leads to a totally uncomplicated schema where the forces of light and darkness ply their trade in a Manichean way.

The first point of departure is in the treatment of mental illness. Nearly all of the villains in this institution for the criminally insane are regarded (by the storyline) as mad, bad, and dangerous to know. They are all considered to be responsible for their actions irrespective of their madness. In this respect, Arkham—in a fictionalized New York City called Gotham—resembles a British mental hospital such as Broadmoor. This establishment was erected in Berkshire in the 1850s as the prototypical institution for the criminally insane—even though such descriptions are studiously avoided.

All of the super-villains contained herein—the Joker, Two-Face, Crock, Black-mask, Doctor Destiny, the Mad Hatter, the Scarecrow, Clay Face, Maxie Zeus, Tweedle-Dum and Tweedle-Dee, Professor Milo, etc.—are all held to be accountable for their crimes, but treatable. This accords with the liberal-humanist notion (based on Pelagianism) that Man is naturally good, rational, kind, humane, and non-criminal. The facts of Man's post-animalian state completely militate against this, of course, but don't forget that we're dealing with an ideology here.

Several psychotherapists are employed in the institution in order to treat the maniacs contained therein. When the lunatics take over the asylum (quite literally), some of them even volunteer to remain with their charges. They have a responsibility, you see.

Just like in a real hospital, a range of treatments (whether medical or ideological) is tried: paint-spot/Rorschach tests, word association mind-games, as well as classic Freudianism — whereas some of the other "therapies" are obviously from the Behavioral school. The director of the institution even uses severe ECT (Electro-Convulsive Therapy) on the "patients." This is interesting for two reasons: one, the anti-psychiatric movement campaigned against this from the 1960s onwards; and, two, it indicates the biological basis of mental illness. It can only be physically assailed if it is somatic to begin with.

In fact, those who are criminally insane fall into two large categories. The offences that they commit — murder, rape, cannibalism, etc. — tend to be rather similar, but the originating conditions are very distinct. The two categories are psychopathia and schizophrenia. Interestingly, the word psychopath (reduced to "psycho" in popular language) is now deeply "offensive" or politically incorrect. It has got to the point that certain staff in these hospitals can be disciplined if they make use of it.

Psychopathia is a birth condition — that is, persons suffering from an advanced personality disorder are born and not made. Psychopaths begin torturing animals about age of four to six and then proceed onto young children later. They regard killing their own species as the equivalent of swatting a fly. Likewise, for them rape is normal sex. It appears that psychopaths are hard-wired to believe that life happens to be a constant war zone of each against all . . . and that love is hatred, quite literally.

They are relatively incapable of lying, unlike normal humans who are mendacious all the time. (Note: this is usually to survive social situations without conflict.) Psychopaths live for conflict, believe life to be worthless, and have utter contempt for social workers, parole board types, concerned professors, and do-gooders who attempt to help them. They often advocate the harshest punishments for criminals of their sort (excluding possibly themselves); they would love to apply such indignities with the maximum amount of torture or humiliation. Psychopaths lack certain female chromosomes (if male) which soften the ferocity of the male nature and prepare it for camaraderie, fatherhood, paternalism, and the softer virtues.

One of the most famous psychopaths in criminology was Peter Kürten (the basis for Fritz Lang's film *M*) who was executed in Germany in the early 1930s. This occurred during that authoritarian halfway house period (typified by a whiff of Conservative Revolutionism) between the end of Weimar and Hitler's rise.

The Joker is certainly a psychopath, but in *Arkham Asylum* he is presented as suffering from Tourette's syndrome. This is a clever notion, because Tourette's is a complicated diagnosis with both positive and negative characteristics. (Mozart is believed to have suffered from it, for instance.) The simplistic thing to say is that Tourette's is a tic-based condition which is both genetic and inherited (i.e., strictly biological). The Joker's mindless and repetitive desire to be rude, upset social order, utter blasphemies, and be mentally sadistic (whilst grinning inanely) are all part and parcel of it.

Yet, if we probe deeper, the Joker can also be diagnosed as suffering from Super Sanity: his ego is completely suppressed, and experience washes over him continuously. He has no filter in relation to hyper-reality (in other words) and is therefore incapable of a conservative gesture; whether linguistically, morally, violently, sexually, etc. Everything is in the moment — he is a pure Existentialist without remit or prior expectancy. With him, Being is becoming — to use philosophical language.

He bears a strong resemblance — as a result of this — to the personality of Caligula, the mad Roman emperor, as designated in Robert Graves' *I, Claudius* and *Claudius the God*, as well as Albert Camus' absurdist play. To bring it to a point: the Joker, like the Mad God Caligula, can embrace you, flirt with you, assassinate you, and dance with the corpse—while laughing continuously . . . as well as having tears of mock-genuine sadness flowing down his cheeks. "I've done away with my best friend, but he deserved it" would be a typical remark.

Batman, by point of contrast, is everything which is ordered, finite, prior, Right-wing, *a priori*, anti-atheistic (in a metaphysical sense), and Objective . . . philosophically. Bruce Wayne (Batman) is a metaphysical Objectivist, a Fascist; the Joker (by dint of contrast) is an anarchist. Yet anarchism and fascism are tied together by virtue of their dialectical inversions of one another. Scratch Nietzsche and you move to Stirner (in the center of this spectrum); scratch Stirner and you end up with the individualistic element in Bakunin, for example. You can also go back along the spectrum as well.

Another consideration arises: the notion of the anarcho-fascist or Right-wing anarchist (a combination of Batman and the Joker). This would include a great number of artists, such as Céline, D. H. Lawrence, Wyndham Lewis, Gottfried Benn, Ernst Jünger, Yukio Mishima, Drieu La Rochelle, T. E. Lawrence, Ezra Pound, and so forth. A new conundrum also arises here: most far Right leaders (unlike the majority of their followers) exhibit Anarch traits, the most notorious political artist of the 20th century being Adolf Hitler, of course. (Note: the supporters of such movements tend to be much more conservative than their leaders, *per se*; they look to such individuals to provide the rebellious conformism, aggressive normalcy, and transgressive stoicism that the Right needs.)

But if we might return to *Arkham Asylum* proper: one of the other major tropes is the treatment of homosexuality. Interestingly, the writer, a Scottish creator called Grant Morrison, wished to visualize the Joker as an effeminate (if threatening) transvestite replete with French bodice and underwear. This is to accentuate the grinning red lips, green hair, palsied or blanched skin, string tie, purple jacket and slacks, and green dress shirt of the original. To link inversion with a psychopathic clown (i.e., a negative image) is relatively reckless on Morrison's part . . . given that any such treatment would be considered "politically incorrect."

In Italian neorealist cinema after the Second World War (for instance) two lesbians were used as a dark or sinister portrayal of fascism, but negative depictions of inversion are rare in contemporary media. (This is contrary to the liberal-Left view that "homophobia" lurks as an omnipresent catch-all.) The last sinister depiction which I can recall is the triumvirate of villains in the Humphrey Bogart version of *The Maltese Falcon*. This starred, quite memorably, Sidney Greenstreet as the eponymous Fat Man. I remember a bourgeois Marxist catalog from the 1980s at the National Film Theatre (in Britain) describing the villainous troupe's portrayal as an example of "bigotry."

Nonetheless, Morrison's schemata for the Joker continues — with him embodying an inverted sadism in contrast to Batman's gruff, no-nonsense, Josef Thorak-laced, and straight as an arrow sensibility.

There are also some terrific scenes in this *folie à deux* (so to say); one of which occurs at the end of the piece. In this particular, Batman starts wrecking the asylum with an axe, and, as he does so, one of the maniacs runs down various corridors (in this Bedlamite labyrinth, you understand) screaming "the Bat — the Bat; he's destroying *everything!*" To which Black-mask responds, "You see, Joker; he's too powerful, you should never have let him in here."

In a great panel, drawn and painted by Dave McKean, the Joker screams as a false martyr: "That's it! Go on, blame me, go on . . . do!" All of this is accompanied by the quiff of emerald hair and the manic smile — amid tons of greasepaint — which just grins on and on without mirth. Just how far the author, Morrison, is aware of any symmetry with Otto Weininger's *Sex and Character* is a moot point, however. In his own mind, he is probably trying to create the "wildest" version of Batman on record, nothing more.

In finality, *Arkham Asylum* goes quite a long way towards considering Batman as a putative Superman (in a Nietzschean sense). First of all, he has to overcome distaste at going in the place to begin with; then he must confront his own "demons" — by virtue of the mentally questionable state of someone who dresses up as a bat in order to beat up criminals for a living. Also, Batman seems hesitant in the face of the Joker's triumphant lunacy inside the Asylum where he can posture as the Lord of Misrule. In one revealing moment he refers to an Arkham run by lunatics as the "real world." Presumably, in this context, the world outside the gates superintended by Commissioner Gordon is unreal.

Nevertheless, Batman goes through a series of tests — even a crucifixion *manqué* — as he gradually conquers the place and subdues it to his will. Over time he sidesteps Harvey Dent's (Two-Face's) deconstruction from dualism, beats down upon Clayface's disease, refuses the nightmares of Doctor Destiny, or the serendipity of Professor Milo. Likewise, he emerges from the Scarecrow's cell unscathed and confronts the man-alligator, Croc, in a clash of the Titans. Yet, throughout the whole process, he is getting stronger and stronger . . . as he engages in personal transcendence or self-over-becoming. Until, by the end of this film on paper, he can absorb the insanity of the place, sublimate it, purge it, throw it forward, and then clamber out on top of it.

By the time the drama ends, Batman makes a move to rejoin the waiting police (headed by Gordon) and the media outside. The criminal lunatics remain inside where they belong, but in a strangely subdued way. The fascistic hero may have lanced the boil (granted), but he has only been able to do so by reintegration, fanaticism for a cause outside oneself, and the adoption of a strength greater than reason. At the end (al-though sane) he has incorporated part of the Joker's Tarot (The Fool or The Hanged Man) into his own purview.

To use an Odinic or pagan device, he is walking with Weird or embracing his own Destiny (fate) — i.e., the will which lies at the end of the road where you will the end's refusal. In this state — perhaps — a fictionalized variant on the end of the Charlemagne Division exists. Remember: they fought on to the end in a fire-torn Berlin because they had no country of their own to return to.

It is intriguing to point out the states which a form of entertainment for children can begin to approach. But it's only a funny book, isn't it?

Counter-Currents/*North American New Right*,
December 31, 2010

The Incredible Hulk

The Incredible Hulk is a Marvel comic which has been running for nigh on 50 years in a relatively unchanged format. In this review I will concentrate on liberal and illiberal or authoritarian and libertarian strands which coexist within it. Most people are dimly aware (if only from Hollywood's version) of Doctor Bruce Banner's transformation into a green behemoth and fighting machine as a result of his exposure to gamma radiation from an atomic bomb test.

What interests me here is less the wraparound — the late Major Talbot, Betty Ross and her father, the indefatigable "Thunderbolt" Ross (General), the adolescent and "hip" sidekick Rick, and so on — than a relationship between Banner and his nemesis. This is the eponymous figure known as the Leader. Like the Hulk, the Leader is green and results from the exposure of an intellectually challenged workman to gamma radiation in the work environment.

The original script which introduced the Leader was drawn by the incomparable Steve Ditko — who hardly ever drew anything other than Spiderman and Doctor Strange for Marvel — and features some charming early moments. For, after the explosion at work, the unnamed laborer experiences painful headaches and an endless desire to read. Indeed, one of the panels shows a nurse staggering with the number of textbooks which this new brain-worker requires in order to keep up with the academic times.

Soon enough, however, the transformation sets in, and the worker is transformed into the Leader — whose distinguishing feature is a long, sloping skull within which his enormous new brain has to fit. Perhaps it is a dolichocephalic one, after the fashion of Conan Doyle's Sherlock Holmes?

The Leader soon decides that, due to his "brainiac" impulses, he and no-one else should be running this planet. The Leader's attempts at world conquest lead to repeated confrontations with Bruce Banner/the Hulk, who thwarts him.

Like all Marvel titles, there is a humanist ethos running through the comic, but it can be undercut by vigilantism, the heroic ideal, and various experiments with tragic characters who defy dualist morals, such as Doctor Doom. The Leader rarely falls under this criterion, but his interest in intellectuality for its own sake raises him above the common ruck of super-villains.

The dialectic between the Hulk and the Leader essentially boils down to brain versus brawn. The Leader possesses a relatively puny body and has to rely upon a series of androids (or even better, Super-androids) to make up the difference between himself and the Hulk's *mass*.

To examine this duality I will be making use of the glossy 400th edition of *The Incredible Hulk* which contains two episodes which feature both main characters in green. (The origin story of the Leader, drawn by Ditko, was appended at the end of this edition.) In this story the Leader is attempting to tap the spirituality of a genuine evangelical leader. He has promised Rick that he will revive his dead girlfriend. And he runs an underground city which is a sort of testing station. He has also connived at a genuine atrocity involving wiping out 4,000 people in a neighboring test city.

This is quite unusual. The villains in comics rarely commit destructive acts—they talk a great deal about doing so, but it remains a rhetoric of power that never approaches your Yugoslav warlord, say. Perhaps revealing the Leader as a species of war criminal (so to say) is to add a genuine *frisson* to the concept of intellectual villainy.

On the Hulk's side, an enormous transformation has occurred. The monster now exists 24/7 but possesses Bruce Banner's intelligence and personality. This happens to be a complete reversal of hundreds of issues of the early Hulk in which the man in green, his clothing splitting around him, was presented as semi-moronic. Logically speaking, the Hulk should always trump the Leader, because he possesses brains plus brawn now, but the Leader always has his devices—robots and 'droids—to even up the score.

In this particular comic book, a mysterious soothsayer called

Agamemnon reveals the existence of the Leader's secret city to Banner, who takes leave of Betty to exact vengeance. Unlike in the early issues, Betty and Bruce are now man and wife. She has become blonde rather than brunette and happens to be married to a gigantic Atlas of a creature who's *green*. I suppose the retention of Bruce Banner's personality is the key enabling factor here.

Towards the end of this graphic novel, an enraged and humanist Hulk becomes more and more ferocious, violent, and blood-curdling — just like his old self. This involves him coming perilously close to the mindless Hulk of all of those prior issues. (This comic appeared in 1992 and the series originated thirty years before in 1962.) It is noticeable that the Hulk's rage is enhanced by the possibility of humanist vengeance for the 4,000, something the Leader seems blithely indifferent to.

This final conflict — to use a third positionist term — is made all the more complicated by the presence of some freakish mutants in the Leader's city, as well as by the intervention of Hydra. (Note: Hydra — like A.I.M. — are fascistic conspiracies in the Marvel universe whose aim is world domination. They contrast — as collective entities — with more individualized villainy elsewhere.) Of course, nothing can withstand the brute power of the Hulk — and it is always necessary for the Leader to escape to fight another day, but he must be vanquished.

All superheroes are elitist and non-humanist figures who fight for Humanist values against elitist figurines (the villains) who fight on behalf of power morality. The villains never refer to themselves as such but instead speak of their *power lordship*. In the case of the Leader, his desire to rule is fostered by his intellectual superiority to all those around him.

The idea also remains latent that extreme mental ability can lead to moral inferiority — when, in fact, it may be the expression of a different ethical viewpoint. This is made much more evident in equivocal villains such as the post-Golden Age Submariner and Doctor Doom. They often teamed up to express this equivocation of being heroic villains or amoral potentates.

For the Leader to win and establish his dictatorship of the led — however — you would not just need to be reading a distinct comic from a rival firm, no, you would have to be living in a different type of society. But everything can change: I have a very early Hulk in the British Fleetway annual from 1972, and it features a moronic Frankenstein in green whose bipolar opposite is Doctor Bruce Banner with whom he alternates.

So, in the annals of fantasy graphics, everything is mutable and subject to change—indeed, the whole Marvel cosmos (now purchased by Disney) is an alternative or parallel universe to begin with. Maybe the Leader's cult of Mind against Mass is not over yet.

Counter-Currents/*North American New Right*
July 9, 2011

JUDGE DREDD

Judge Dredd is *the* publishing phenomenon of British comics for the last 30 years, if not more. Nearly all of the strips have been written by John Wagner under his own name and a variety of aliases, while a great number of artists have worked on the sequences.

For this lantern-jawed Judge (part policeman, part vigilante, part judge, part jury) contains almost ludicrously denied fascistic undercurrents which only pedants bother to deny. Dredd's personality and physiology never alters—he is the same from the first strip to the last—and the fact that he never develops but always remains unchanging is part of the character's *esprit*. The graphic novel is a satire which can be read "straight," and hence we detect its dangers for liberal orthodoxy. This has been commented on many times—that somehow, read as black farce, a "fascist" comic, no matter how unintentionally, has enjoyed massive sales and influence in non-compliance with Politically Correct norms.

Essentially the Judges are the last defense against complete chaos and irretrievable social breakdown. They are the morally efficacious governing elite which runs Mega-City One—an enormous version of New York which sprawls across North America and contains tens of millions of citizens. The city is virtually a state (or city-state) in its own right.

The Judges are police, jury, judge, and executioner all rolled into one. Each Judge spends 10, 12, or 14 years in training—they never retire (except to teach law in the staff college) or to go into mutant land, badlands full of radiation, which exist beyond the city's precincts. There they go to bring law to the lawless. This leads to quite hilarious breakdowns in liberal jurisprudence—such as when Dredd says to a trembling malcontent under his boot: "Obey me; obey the law!"

All of the Judges fly helicopter gunships and use super-powered bikes. They are also heavily armored and carry every type of weaponry. They are ready to die and give their lives for the City. They are a Praetorian Guard, if you will. A Supreme or Chief Judge is elected by the others to lead the judges, and psychic phenomena are terribly real—they are part of routine life, hence a deputation of "psi" Judges who are in position to deal with them.

At best, this comic strip obeys a type of ultra-conservatism that stretches PC norms but just about remains within them. There are occasional homilies about inclusion—but these tend to relate to persons mutated by radiation rather than the usual PC constituencies. There is a relative absence of liberal lecturing—presumably because the form is considered too low and populist to really be worth bothering with.

Obviously the bulk of the readership consists of adolescent boys of all ages—one imagines that this runs the gamut from 12 to 40 years of age. Action is the key word here—and one is reminded of Raymond Chandler's dictum about pulp fiction; namely, when one is in doubt about a plot, just have an armed man enter the room. Judge Dredd is very much along these lines. A vast variety of plots have occurred over the years, but, in order to give a flavor of them, I have decided to concentrate on one extended story which is a quarter of a century old.

The story in question was known as *The Executioner* and was based on a speed view of a forgettable VHS video from the '80s called *The Exterminator*. The story was 26 pages in length and featured a beautiful female vigilante called Blanche Tatum who sets out to revenge her husband's death. He was driven to suicide by threats from a criminal gang who offered him a loan under loan shark terms.

The story pivots around the fact that she was a rookie Judge later expelled from college for dating her future husband. Her skills as a Judge are put into good effect in assassinating a range of criminal lowlifes—they tend to meet a fate which is appropriate to their criminal career or demeanor.

Judge Dredd gradually gets closer and closer to the perpetrator ("perp" in Judges' slang). The woman is presented in glamorous if understated terms . . . she is a thin blonde, blue-eyed, who wears facial jewelry, blue lipstick, and an Alice band that sweeps her hair back over her forehead. In her guise as the Executioner, she wears a black ninja suit plus a hooded mask. Her signature or calling card is a small handbill with JUSTICE IS DONE printed upon it.

The real twist in the story isn't the action or the violence, but, rather, the coincidence between the proto-Judge as a vigilante and the fact that, under liberal jurisprudence, the Judges are virtually vengeance mongers themselves. It is this tension between the pseudo-Judge and the real Judges which makes the story work, or adds depth to it, at any rate.

The story of Blanche Tatum helps to expose part of the reality of Judgeship. In the end, just like a male Western hero, Blanche sends the children to the grandparents and goes looking for the final loan shark perpetrators to take out with her violent handbills. Having done so, she dies in the end at the hands of Judge Dredd, but only because her weapon had no ammunition left. This "Judge" who reveals the reality of Judgeship has no aptitude for taking on her own former colleagues.

Interestingly, opinion polls in Mega-City One reveal a 95% approval rating for the vigilante. Only 1% is against—including Judge Dredd. In his pithy remark: "Justice it may be; legal it ain't!"

It probably applies to the Judge Dredd brand as a whole.

Counter-Currents/*North American New Right*
July 7, 2011

Blind Cyclops:
The Strange Case of
Dr. Fredric Wertham

In 1954, an obscure psychiatrist penned a book called *Seduction of the Innocent* which almost put paid to the entire comic book industry in the United States. The whole incident is almost forgotten today, but it is highly instructive over how "firestorms" and cultural wars can break out. It is also reasonably true to say that—unlike the parallel film industry—it took American comics about three decades to fully ingest and recover from Doctor Wertham's assault.

Fredric Wertham was an Ashkenazic psychiatrist who basically applied half-digested ideas from social anthropology to the cultural realm. He definitely believed that many of the tearaways and juvenile delinquents that he had to deal with in the late 1940s and early 1950s were the products of bad culture.

It's instructive to point out that Wertham doesn't seem to import any information from other disciplines or clusters of ideas. Like Boas and Margaret Mead, he believes that Man is totally socially conditioned when almost the opposite is true. Strongly influenced by real criminal cases, Wertham believed that young louts and hoodlums were the actual product of their violent "reading" material.

This is almost completely base about apex. It was true that reform school types majored on pulps, irregular 'zines—the subliminal pornography of that era—and violent comic books. Many of the latter were published by Entertainment Comics (EC), owned by William Gaines, whose firm was virtually forced out of business as a result of Wertham's fiat.

It is important to realize that a small proportion of Wertham's assertions were true, at least from a socially conservative perspective. About 5% of these comics or graphic novels depicted quite considerable sadism (eye-gouging, etc.) and tacitly sexual imagery. It is also true that such material was unashamedly targeted at minors, children, and young adults. Most parents instinctively believe that the escapist material which the young like to peruse is harmful—and a small proportion of it doubtless is.

But what Wertham doesn't understand (on largely ideological grounds) is that mankind's nature proves to be biologically grounded—the social and environmental attributes of which are themselves tributaries of genetics. Goaty youths want to peruse violent, forceful, imaginative, masculinist, and heroic material in order to escape from an often humdrum existence. It is doubtless correct, however, that those with a psychopathic personality will be attracted to material that ramifies with their deepest urges.

The publication of Doctor Wertham's *Seduction of the Innocent* led to his appearance before the Senate Subcommittee on Juvenile Delinquency and the decimation of the comics industry thereafter. Many of these comics were completely harmless, in my view—the majority of their themes were Gothic staples akin to Isak Dinesen's *Seven Gothic Tales*, or the works of Ambrose Bierce, Arthur Machen, and Edgar Allan Poe. The bulk of them would quite easily have provided scripts or (more accurately) storyboards for *The Twilight Zone* and other series in the '50s.

Nonetheless, due to the overwhelming ethnicity of those who founded the comics industry, a subtle "liberal" bias pervades. The touch (at this historical period) is extremely light, but anti-racism, a trace of anti-McCarthy feeling, anti-anti-Semitism, hostility to any type of color bar, a certain anti-police rhetoric, and an unheroic attitude to military service all prevail.

The latter point is quite interesting. In contrast to the virulent patriotism of Sergeants Fury and Rock at Marvel and DC later on, EC comics were pacifist, dead-beat, and cynical. It's almost as if there attitude was more redolent of an anti-Vietnam war comic like *War is Hell*—even an ultra-cynical piece like Dalton Trumbo's *Johnny Got His Gun*. (This piece of agitprop, in artistic guise, goes right back to early Communist anti-war art, on the German side, after the Great War. This involved brochures or picture books which depicted soldiers who had been dreadfully maimed at the front. The Nietzschean response would be to commit suicide; the Leftist one to exhibit the maimed.)

Wertham's views were subtly different from all of this, however. Despite sharing the "soft Left" or Jewish humanist mindset of EC (up to a point), he saw things in a much wider way. After all, his intervention led to the self-imposed Comics Code (for fear of state intervention), as well as the destruction of hundreds of thousands of comics by state troopers in the '50s. Some grainy black-and-white photos from this decade still survive.

It is interesting to note that much of the indictment of one particular government in the 20th century—book burning; persecution of modernist art; eugenics and dysgenics in psychiatric hospitals, etc.—all occurred in virtually every Western society. This includes Sweden, Britain, and the United States, where far Right movements were all conspicuously unsuccessful.

Bloated with success, Wertham attempted to "clean up" early television in the same way. But he was picking on a much larger, better financed, and more resilient industry here. It also possessed much more influential political backers and friends. His anti-televisual thesis, *War on Children* (1959) couldn't find a publisher, and Wertham's cultural influence subsequently waned.

His response was to become even more hysterical and sidelined, however. In his fringe published book in 1966, *A Sign for Cain*, Wertham declared that the increasing violence, grotesquerie, desensitization, and commercial "paganism" of mass media was laying the grounds for a new Holocaust. This was an extraordinary claim when taken at face value!

Yet Wertham was tapping into something—like Christian evangelicals and puritan campaigners of the time—who realized that generic media is a factor of 20 to 50 times more violent, explicit, sensual, sub-pornographic, and "uncensored" now than when I was born in 1962. Despite having campaigned for this "liberation," many liberals are secretly uneasy about what they have unleashed—particularly if they settle down to have children in mid-life. But it's too late now!

Put rather tritely, what Wertham and Co. misunderstand is Man's dual nature. Most normal or well-adjusted people instinctively feel that children should be protected from low-grade material. Nonetheless, when it comes to adolescent and adult works, there is then a cultural war over the meaning of fare that oscillates between Eros and Thanatos. Humans are violent and erotic beings—this will manifest itself in culture.

You either have Shakespeare's *King Lear*, replete with Gloucester's blinding scene with Cornwall, or you have the Marxist equivalent of the play, Edward Bond's *Lear*, containing, as it does, Bond's eye-removing machine. The latter is a counter-cultural testament to the utilitarianism of cruelty. The struggle is to decide whether you have one variant or the other; *and what it means*.

At a much lower cultural level, does a Marvel comic like the *Black Panther* subliminally preach what Obama's wife really thinks about the American Union; or does the revolutionary English Puritan *Solomon Kane*, another Marvel title from Robert E. Howard touched up by Roy Thomas, exemplify the glories of an Aryan warrior (Howard's own words in one of his stories—a language use which was excised from a version printed in the late '60s in Czechoslovakia)?

Wertham himself declined later to a stumbling apologia for comics fandom, at least in terms of the fanzines which they produced themselves. These obviously didn't contain the violent, mastodonic, and sensual material of which he disapproved. This work, *The World of Fanzines* (1974), attempted to reconcile him with a middle-aged clientele for graphic novels that viewed him with considerable hostility. There was even a revenge against him from within the community of fandom, *Doctor Wirtham's Comix and Stories* (1979), which admitted that he was right.

An age of Horror awaits us all . . . ?

Counter-Currents/*North American New Right*
December 1, 2010

Robert E. Howard
& the Heroic[*]

I'll be talking about Robert Ervin Howard. A while back, I had a talk about H. P. Lovecraft, Aryan mystic, and he was one of a triumvirate of writers who wrote for a fantasy magazine called *Weird Tales*, a pulp magazine; they were incredibly cheaply produced magazines in the 1930s, with quite good art, graphic sort of art, printed on cheap bulk newsprint paper which was very acidic and fell apart very quickly.

And yet three writers, Clark Ashton Smith, Robert Ervin Howard, and Howard Phillips Lovecraft have survived and been inducted into literature. I saw in my local library that Penguin Classics, or Modern Classics, the ones with the gray covers, now include Robert Ervin Howard's *Heroes in the Wind, from Kull to Conan: The Best of Robert E. Howard* as a book. Penguin Classics, you see? So it begins as a pulp, and a hundred years later it's redesignated as literature.

Howard is a very interesting figure. He only lived 30 years. He was born in 1906 and shot himself with a revolver in the head in his car, outside his home, when he was 30 years of age. We'll get on to that afterwards. He wrote 160 stories, and the interesting thing about these stories is that they are pre-civilized in their settings; they're barbaric; they're ultra-masculine stories; and they deal with many themes which have been so disprivileged from much of mainstream liberal humanist culture that they no longer exist.

Howard had a range of heroes and wrote in most popular

---

[*] Transcription by John Morgan and V. S. of a lecture entitled "Robert Ervin Howard: Pulpster Extraordinaire," given at the 26th New Right meeting in London on Saturday April 17, 2010.

Two digressions have been removed, but the uncut audio version and complete transcript are available online at Counter-Currents: http://www.counter-currents.com/2013/06/robert-e-howard-and-the-heroic-complete/

genres. He wrote to make money, but he began as a poet, and a poetic and sort of Saturnalian disposition influenced his work and his friendship, by correspondence, with Lovecraft, and to a lesser extent, Clark Ashton Smith, throughout his life.

He was of Irish descent, and he was born in a town which became a boom town in the oil booms of the early 20th century in Texas. For those of you who don't know, Texas is enormous. England fits into Texas twelve times, and Britain, eight times. He was born in Peaster, Texas, and spent some of his early life in a town called Brownwood, a quintessentially small-town American, which is the experience of most white Americans through the settlement of Western civilization in North America. The state capital, of course, is Austin, and you have the big cities like Houston, Dallas, and Galveston.

Now, Howard hated the oil booms, and what happened. When the oil boom happened, Cross Plains, a town of about 1,200 with a mayor and so on, morphed into a large, sprawling, lawless place of about 10,000. An enormous number of prospectors and drillers and criminals and people seeking easy money, all heavily armed of course, came into Cross Plains. The town burst out beyond its limits in all directions. Oil was discovered everywhere. Fortunes were made, and fortunes were lost.

At the time he was born, lynchings were still in vogue right across the South and the ex-Confederate states. Everyone displayed and carried weapons openly. Sometimes the Rangers, as they were called, a man alone in the sun with a rifle, was basically all you had of semi-ordered civilization. People don't realize how, if you like, wild and open certain parts of the United States were, certainly until the 1860s, 1870s.

The psychological experience of an intuitive and sympathetic and radically imaginative young man like Howard invests the tall Texan story, and stories of prospectors and ranchers and drillers in the oil industry, and Texas Rangers and Marshals and so on, with an added piquancy. His family supported the Confederacy in a previous generation, and he was mildly descended from certain Confederate commanders.

His attitude towards life is expressed in the stories, which is why they survived. The stories are like lucid dreams. You walk straight into them, and the action begins. Most of them were dreams, and in a way, most critics believe Howard's an oral creator. He's in the oral, folklorist, and narrative-oriented tradition. He's a storyteller *par excellence*. It's said he wrote at night, and he used to chant the stories to himself, which of course is a very old Northern European and Nordic tradition. It's the idea of the *skald*. It's the idea that things are illuminated to you, and you speak because you hear the voice.

He had a series of masculine heroes beginning with certain Celtic and Pictish/Scotch-Irish heroes such as Bran Mak Morn and so on; Conan, the hero that he's most associated with, whose name, of course, is abstracted from Sir Arthur Conan Doyle's middle name. Howard would take from all sorts of roots, many of which related to heroic, Celtic, Indo-European elements which he imagined to exist in his own past.

He was very influenced by G. K. Chesterton's dictum at the beginning of the 20th century that myth is the commingling of emotional reality with what is understood to be fact. If you mix together eras and peoples, but you keep the emotional truth of the substance of what we perceive their lives to have been, then you can influence the present and the future. It's noumenal truth, as Aristotle said 2,000 years ago, the idea that certain things are artistically and emotionally true irrespective of what you think about them factually.

His most famous series of stories, the Conan stories that he wrote pretty much towards the end of his life, were based upon a false yet true/factual world history, the so-called Hyborian Age that he created for himself. Maps of the Hyborian Age have been produced, and they are based upon a realistic sociology, ethnography, geological history, and a coherent view of economics. The country of Aquilonia that Conan ends up conquering at the end of the mythos is partly Britain. The Picts are partly the Scots, of course, covered in woad, barbaric, kept out by a wall, that sort of thing.

War is the dynamic of all of Howard's fiction, and his attitude towards life was conflict-oriented. His stories are described as ultra-masculine and non-feminist stories. Unkind critics say that they're Barbara Cartland for men, where all women are beautiful, all men are heroic, where magic works instead of science, and where force decides all social problems, and there is a degree to which the genre which he has founded, called sword and sorcery — of which one supposes J. R. R. Tolkien, an Oxford professor, is the senior representative in the 20th century — is an example of the literary and the heroic in contemporary letters. It's interesting to notice that the early great texts of the Western civilization, Homer, *Beowulf*, are deeply heroic, and yet over time, the heroic imprimatur within our language and within our sensibility dips.

It's said that boys aren't interested in reading at school, and that 80 to 90% of those who do English literature courses in further educational colleges and universities, the tertiary sector, are women. It's said that men disprivilege literature, and it's also said in the West that boys get bullied if they're regarded, as Howard was when he was younger, as sissies because they read too much, and this sort of thing.

I think one of the problems is that literature that appeals to men is often not the concern of the people who run these sorts of educational establishments. If the sort of people that influenced Howard, people like Noyes, people like Robert W. Service, people like Byron, people like Kipling, people like the heroic imperialist literature of William Henley, who was the basis for Long John Silver in *Treasure Island*, and was a close friend of Robert Louis Stevenson, a man who could go from bonhomie to murderous rage with a click of your fingers, as Silver does in *Treasure Island*, of course, because he moves from extreme malevolence to a sort of Cockney paternalism in the same breath. Now, if this literature was normative much further down the social and the educational scale, one would imagine that boys and youngish men would be much more interested in literature as a whole.

Howard essentially sold stories from about the age of 20, certainly 19. He started writing when he was 9, and the interesting thing about him is that his stories are not really derivative. There are connections to enormous writers that were prominent at the time, principally Jack London, but Howard emerged fully formed and had his own voice from the very beginning.

London's a very interesting figure, because London's often been associated, truthfully and yet falsely, with the extreme Left. Trotsky, of course, wrote an introduction to his famous dystopia of American life called *The Iron Heel*. And yet London, as George Orwell intimated in one of his essays, was proto-fascistic, and was in many ways a Left nationalist, or even a National Bolshevik, or somebody who would be now described as a Third Positionist. London's positions were those of socialism from the outside, but also a form of socialism, with and without quotation marks, that was Right-wing rather than Left-wing, and was both national and racial. The interesting thing about London's discourse is the radicalism of the racialism and the almost completely disavowed anti-Semitism which was a part of that.

Literature a hundred years ago could be written with a degree of freedom in relation to ethnic, racial, and sociobiological matters which is now unthinkable. It's not just that Political Correctness polices the grammar of what people think and write. It's that to many people who receive a higher liberal education — and obviously the bulk of writers of the present and the future will be such people — even to have such thoughts is regarded as "unthinkable."

It's interesting to notice that if you go to Wikipedia and scale down the long, and quite interesting, biographical information about Howard, who's considered to be a major figure because there's 40 million hits on the internet about him and that sort of thing, and he's one of these people who wrote earlier in the 20th century that the masses are actually interested in. Yet the interesting thing is that if you scroll down to the middle of the Wikipedia section it says "Racism — Problematical Attitudes Towards Race in the Fiction of Robert E. Howard." There's another section underneath that: "Sexism and Feminism."

So, any writer basically before about 1950, and most mainstream cinema — which of course has often revolved around romance and the heroic, as its two pillars, if you like — a lot of Western cinema before 1960, even quite a lot of Hollywood product, is relatively healthy. It's only when you get to the extraordinary self-hatred exemplified by culturally Marxist works, say in the early 1970s, like *Soldier Blue*, which is a film largely about the Vietnam War, in which the whites are the villains, Caucasians are sadists, the Indians are the heroic victims of our pitiless racial sadism, and this sort of thing. The complete reversal of the "Cowboy and Indian" metaphysic that had survived in the Western from the earliest Westerns that were done as silent films in the 1920s.

The spirit of Howard is much closer to the figure of a very early giant of Hollywood cinema who was called D. W. Griffith, who was a Texan like himself, and who made in 1915 the two-part *Birth of a Nation*. *Birth of a Nation*, which you can get, available everywhere on video, and which is a film that appears to be superficially humorous now because it's so transgressive. Can you imagine a film where the Klan is the hero? And the Confederacy is regarded as a neutral to goodish to morally benign force? And where the carpetbagger politicians, with their descendants' descendants' descendant in the White House now, are the villains?

[...]

Now, Howard was a radical Southerner who particularly admired the Texan spirit, the spirit of the tall story, the spirit of an oral literature which is handed down and which is largely concerned with masculine struggles. Money, although he needed it to support his mother who was dying of cancer throughout his life, was of little consequence to Howard, although about the time that the Great Depression hit in '29, '30, '31, Howard earned more than any other man in Cross Plains, including the bank manager.

Although he lost all of his savings, as most of the people in south and mid-Texas did, because every bank went down in 1929/1930. The bank which Howard had all his money in from the early stories collapsed, and he put it in another bank quickly. He actually had to queue up in the heat, take the money physically out, stick it in another bank, and then that other bank went down because, of course, the state was not intervening to save these banks, and therefore they all went down.

Bank managers would be pursued out of towns by people with rifles looking for their money physically because the chap was moving with it. And yet the inflation was such that the money was increasingly becoming worthless anyway.

So, Howard lost two minor fortunes and had to rebuild it. Certainly the monetary stress that he and his family suffered from, [and the fact] that he was very close — perhaps unnaturally close, psychologically, to his mother and estranged from his father who was a town physician — contributed to some of the factors that led to his suicide in 1936 at the age of 30.

Howard's attitude towards life in the stories and in terms of his own emotions was pre-modern. He believed that life was essentially heroic, that you should die young, that the future had no promise unless it led to glory, that materialism and the belief that getting on in life is all that's important is something against which he was in rebellion.

He also agreed fundamentally with Spengler, that cultures were cyclical, that the civilization in which he lived . . . Don't forget that he's living in a period in which America was beginning to become the dominant power on earth, yet many people in rural Texas are only dimly aware.

When I visited Texas once, a while back, there would be a newspaper which you can buy in one of these slot machines on the side of the road and you take it out and it says "Foreign News." And foreign news is what's happening in Oklahoma! Europe's on the other side of the moon, you know. And yet, when you look at the size of Texas, the sheer size of it, you know, Britain eight times. To drive from the tip of Cornwall to the top of Scotland and you've only gone a tiny distance within Texas. When you begin to realize these distances and how they play on the mind, what's going on in Canada, what's going on in Oklahoma *is* somewhere else, isn't it? Very radically.

So, many of these attitudes which appear narrow and fundamentalist in various respects (cultural, psychological, political, religious) appear more logical, more in the zone when you're there in the extraordinary heat. One of the things Europeans notice about parts of Texas is that the heat is so intense at times it's almost unbearable. The heat comes off the ground and it hits you like a force. You know, you wear these sorts of hats to stop the back of your neck from being covered in skin cancer. Many of their habits which appear absurd are not so when you're there.

Howard's early stories dealt with the Celtic twilight, probably influenced by Lord Dunsany and Arthur Machen, the Anglo-Welsh horror and Gothic writer who was a member of the Golden Dawn in Britain with W. B. Yeats, Crowley, and various other people; Algernon Blackwood, of course, who contributed a lot to the English ghost story tradition; English Gothic fiction, you might call it higher horror writing, literary horror, that Lovecraft and Poe exemplify in the American tradition, largely in their cases a pure American offshoot of English literature, often written in a slightly archaic English way because many of the old, deeply Protestant 1600s, 1700s ways of using language are current in the United States well into the late 19th and early 20th centuries. This slightly aimless, unfocused American English—this bureaucratic speech of contemporary America, not redolent of their great artists, it has to be said, but the sort of speech that America uses when it speaks to the rest of the world on CNN—that didn't exist then, because the book the North Americans learned was the 1611 version of the Bible.

The Protestant fundamentalism which is a part of the United States' psyche is extraordinarily important, in my view, for any cultural understanding of the white inheritance inside the United States. We had at the meeting before last, a speaker from Croatia called Tomislav Sunić who wrote a book which I edited a long time ago, actually, called *Homo Americanus: Child of the Postmodern Age*. Among the very important points about that book is his recognition, as a European ex-Catholic in his case, of the Protestant fundamentalist nature of the United States. I think this is a crucial point to understand the United States.

The influence of contemporary Jewry in the United States is due to the fact that it's a Protestant fundamentalist country, and many, many Americans really believe in their deep and even subconscious mind that the viewpoint that they are a self-chosen elect to rule by right, by divine imprecation, is so deep in their consciousness, the idea, as Pentecostalists sing, that "we are Zion," goes so far down that the difference between their identity and their group specificity and their militant patriotism and that of a small country in the Middle East, and people who didn't begin to emigrate *en masse* into the United States until the latter stages of the 19th century, and only really began to have major socioeconomic impact, particularly culturally, in the first quarter to a third of the 20th century makes these things, to my mind, easier to understand.

Now, Protestant fundamentalism doesn't seem to have scratched Howard very much, and yet one of his heroes is a Puritan called Solomon Kane, and Solomon Kane, who comes between Bran Mak Morn, Kull, and Conan, is in some ways his first major hero. Solomon Kane is very, very interesting because he's one of these Protestant extremists of the 1620s — well, they're set before — but that's when the movement comes to power in the Cromwellian Interregnum in England, and yet stretches way back into the previous century, and yet in a strange way he's an outsider, even in that movement.

Kane dresses all in black with a little white sort of a bib round his neck. He's extraordinarily heavily armed, as most of the Puritans were, had a sword on either side, had pistols in the belts, had a knife in the boot, because you were fighting for *the Lord*, you see! "I am the flail of the Lord." They had these endless quotes, largely from the Old Testament, but to a degree from elements of the New, which they would roll out on occasions when they had to justify what they were about to do, and that their instincts wanted to do, in a way that nothing could restrain them.

There's a famous moment in Northern Ireland, when James Callaghan was Northern Irish Secretary under Wilson in the late 1960s, slightly sympathetic to Social Democratic, Catholic nationalism in Northern Ireland, as part of the Labour movement was then, but in a very moderate way, and he said in a concerned and perplexed way to the Reverend Ian Paisley — who softened a bit as he's got older, and in turn wanted to be Prime Minister of Northern Ireland before he died — he said to

Paisley, "But we're all the children of God, Reverend," and Paisley said, "No! Nooooo!" He said, "We are the children of *wrath!*"

And that is the attitude of those Puritan extremists, loyal to the Old Testament in many ways. Men of a sort of always implacable fury, and elements of their dictatorship, under Cromwell of course, were increasingly maniacal. The banning of Shakespeare, our greatest writer. When an English national revolutionary movement bans the country's greatest-ever writer, you do begin to think there's something slightly wrong, don't you, no? Similarly, the flogging of actors under the New Model Army in Newcastle for performing Shakespeare. These were the latter stages. These were the Buddhas of Bamiyan moments, weren't they really, of these English revolutionaries of the 1640s, or what was really going on?

Now, the sort of Puritanism that Howard puts into this character is different, because Howard's character, Solomon Kane, is a loner, a man who always fights for his own cause, but when he hears those almost voluptuous pagan stirrings in the background, it's always Christianized, and it's always put in a Protestant context.

Cromwell once had a phrase: "I disembowel you for Christ's love." And that's what he said in the Putney Debates. When the parliamentary side won the Civil War, the whole New Model Army, which of course was a revolutionary army of that time — no brothels, no drinking; in the Royal army, you went to the back, and there was endless entertainment at the back of the battlefront. With the Puritan armies, there was none of that. You went to the back, and there was no drinking, and there was a chap ranting at you about whether you'd sinned that day.

It was less fun, but at the same time, when they raised their pikes together, not in a higgledy-piggledy way, or one bloke at the back didn't want to, but they raised them *together*, as one unit. They would all chant, "God is our strength."

Cromwell understood as Shaw said early in the 20th century that a man who has a concept of reality that is metaphysically objectivist, a man who believes in something as absolute truth is worth 50 men. And that's the type of revolutionary ideology that these people then had.

But at the Putney Debates, there was a debate about how the country should go, and Ireton and the other supreme commanders were there. Under Cromwell they committed regicide of course, they killed the King, so the future of the country was theirs. There was another tendency known as the Levellers, who in some ways of course were retrospectively the first socialists, so-called because they wanted to level down distinctions. There was an even more radical movement called the Diggers that came along later.

But Cromwell told Ireton, "Either we hang them or they will hang us." And that's the Levellers. And at the end of the Putney Debates, the army moves aside, the Cromwellian regime has been established, and the Levellers are hanging on the trees. So Cromwell had got his way.

The importance of Protestantism to the United States, in a complicated way, is the reason why there has never been an extreme Right-wing movement of any great success in the United States, except in a localized way like the Klan to deal with particular circumstances at a particular time. America, you would imagine, is ripe for such a movement, as Australia always has been, and yet there has not been one, not really. Not a national movement.

There were figures in the 1930s: there was the Silver Shirt movement; there was Father Coughlin's radio broadcasts which had all sorts of interesting ramifications in American life: a Catholic priest giving the radical Right to essentially a Protestant nation, which of course set up a cultural tension and contradiction in and of itself.

There are also interesting liberal counterparts to this. Most people remember Orson Welles' treatment of H. G. Wells' *The War of the Worlds*, where the Martians invade New York, and then he admitted it was a fiction retrospectively, and tens of thousands of ninnies leave New York because they think the Martians are landing. "Gee, they're up the road!" And they get the pickup truck, and they go. And then they broadcast later that it was all a stunt, and it was an artistic show, and people shouldn't take it literally.

Welles deliberately did that to discredit Coughlin. He said afterwards, "We did it because too many people believed everything that fascist priest was telling them on the radio, so we proved them, 'don't believe what you hear that comes out of the radio.'" And that's a purely sort of aesthetic response to the impact that sort of thing had.

Yet still movements lie there: Aryan Nations, National Alliance, these sorts of movements, very small, very isolated, geographically and in other ways. National Alliance was quite interesting because it morphed from Youth for [George] Wallace. That's how it started, and then it took various transformatory steps until it emerged as a very hard-line group under the late Dr. William Pierce at a later date.

And this culture of extreme Protestantism—which contained elements which are to the Right of almost anything you've ever seen, mentally, psychologically, conceptually—seems partly, because, of its extreme individualism, to be incapable of generating radical Right mass movements. Most Americans still adopt a deliberately materialist, liberal humanist and individualist way of looking at life.

They divide into two basic political parties that have switched over during the course of the last two centuries. Don't forget in the 19th century the Republican Party was the party of the nominal Left, and the Democrats were red. The Democrats were conservatives who supported states' rights—not the right to secede, but certainly the right to own slaves. The party led by a man who's proud to have ex-slaves in his own family, the present President, would have actually, in a strange sort of way, not been able to join the Democrat Party in the 19th century, and yet the switch around, that you can vote in each other's primaries, and that "Isn't everyone a Democrat? Isn't everyone a Republican?"—hence the meaninglessness of the names—adds to this sort of feeling that you get in the contemporary United States that all that matters is money and social success. America's very important, because America, of course, dominates this country now culturally and geopolitically. We can't almost do anything without them, and all the wars that we're now dragged into are due to American hegemony.

But the repudiation of parts of American power should never blind ourselves to the cultural excellence of what many white Americans have achieved, both for their group and individually. If you actually look at all the radical Right literature, the alternative side of an isolationist and American nationalist posture, there is some great work there by people like William Gayley Simpson, who wrote an enormous book of over a thousand pages called *Which Way Western Man?*

Again, without going on a tangent too much, he's a very interesting man because he's an ex-Trappist monk, who began as a liberal and an aching humanist whose heart bled for the Third World and who had all the correct sort of UN-specific attitudes, and gradually he changed step by step by step, and he ended up, if not a member then a fellow traveler, of the National Alliance. That is quite a change. That is quite a leap. But it is also true that tens and tens of thousands of educated Western people who are liberal-minded now will have to change their views, will have to begin to change their mindset in this and the coming generation if Western civilization is virtually not to slide off the cliff. [. . .]

Now, to return to Howard: don't forget that he was sort of mature at 22 and dead at 30. He produced 160 stories, 15, 16 volumes basically, and other fragments. There was an unfinished fantasy novel called *Almuric*, the early Celtic stories, Bran Mak Morn and the others morphed into Solomon Kane. There were associated Westerns and humorous stories. There were some detective stories, but he never particularly liked that genre, although his attitude towards life was hard-boiled. There were also some Crusader stories as well, and some slightly mythological stories about a sort of white man in the East called Gordon, presumably named after the Gordon of Khartoum, but actually an American, and these were the old Borak stories set in Afghanistan, where he goes native and fights along sort of intertribal and group-based and clan lines in that context.

Howard's attitude toward politics is quite complicated and not entirely logical and primarily emotional. He supported the

New Deal because he believed the American economy had collapsed and something needed to be done. He argued strongly with H. P. Lovecraft, who was more of a "reactionary" in these respects, a classical liberal, didn't like Roosevelt and the people around him, didn't like intervention in the market in that sort of Protestant, American way. He felt that you fail commercially, *you suffer punishment*, because God has chosen that punishment for you. Destiny involves sacrifice.

The irony is that the banks have been saved in the United States by Bush, costing trillions of dollars, but the metaphysic which founded the country would have allowed all of those banks to fail, all of those banks to fail and all those bankers to hang themselves and throw themselves off buildings. That happened in 1929. And then you rebuild quickly, because the pure, American, sort of Randian view is that capitalism is an insatiable animal and vortex of energy. And if people go to pot, if people lose everything they have, if as a trader ... An insurance agent I vaguely knew years ago at Lloyd's, lost all his money in the Names scandal, and goes there on a Sunday and unlocks the door and goes down to the toilets and sits there and drinks Domestos and kills himself and is found by the cleaners—Africans probably—on Monday morning. And his senior partner in Lloyd's said, "Well, that's capitalism for you." And that's it! What goes up goes down! This was the view that founded the United States.

And yet the irony is, why have these Western politicians intervened? Why have they saved these structures? Few collateral damage moments, Lehman Brothers; they've charged Goldman Sachs with fraud. Well, that's a bit late, isn't it, really? And yet why have they intervened? They've intervened because of the voting danger. The fact that there are radical parties on the fringe of all Western societies—everyone knows who they are—that people could vote for in a major moment of fiscal/physical/moral/emotional distress, and the whole Western clerisy that's bought into the contemporary liberal package knows that. Many of these parties are actually quite moderate in relation to the traditions they come out of, but they *terrify* the present establishment that often sees the more populist ones as just the start of something worse that's coming behind, see?

And there's also a certain guilt there as well, because these people are well aware of what's happened to Western societies because they've been running them for 70 years. This idea it's all an accident, "I didn't really mean it," and the turning of Western societies into a sort of version of Brasília, *en masse* with a tiny, little elite at the top that's creaming most of the goodies off for themselves.

I'm not an egalitarian in any sense, but it's interesting to note that this country's slightly more unequal now than it was in 1910 in terms of 90% of all equity and all capital and all wealth is owned by the top 10%, and the top 2% of that 10%, and yet the society has changed out of all recognition, 1910 to 2010. Most Western people born in the first part of the 20th century would not believe the transformation of the West just in a lifetime, basically, after they died. And it occurred because of the extraordinary wars, largely amongst ourselves, that we fought in the 20th century that also gave outsider ideologies like Communism their chance, vulture-like to pick over the defeat and the carrion corpses of what was left.

The heroic attitude towards man and society that Howard's work depicts exists virtually nowhere except as play and pleasure in computer games for boys and adolescents, in comic books and so on. The areas of life where that sort of ethos remains—the armed forces, the army, navy, and air force of most contemporary Western societies, particularly their specialist or elite forces, in Britain the Special Air service, the naval equivalent the Special Boat Service, and all of those novels, these Andy McNab sort of novels about the heroic and this sort of thing, which are lapped up by a largely male audience, *largely male audience*—other than that, there is not really the imprimatur of the heroic in Western life.

The extraordinary demilitarization of Western life, hardly ever see a policeman, hardly ever see soldiers. When do you ever see British forces? And that's because they're always outside the country as globalist mercenaries fighting American and Zionist wars all over the world. They're never seen here, and many of their commanders don't want them here, either, because they regard parts of British life as so irretrievably decadent that they actually want to keep their troops away from much of what's happened in relation to the society.

There are towns in Berkshire where a lot of the military stay, like Arborfield and these sorts of towns, where it's quite clear there's a sort of military zone and there's a civilian zone. You all know what British towns are like on Friday, Saturday night: no police; they're all in their vans; they're all in the station; they're at home; they're filling in forms. They wear yellow bibs when they're out, but when you want one, you can never see them, can you?

And a lot of our older people are, let's face it, frightened to go into town and city centers on Thursday, Friday, Saturday, certainly after 6. And why is this happening? It's partly happening because the concept that Howard's fiction deals with, masculinity, has been completely disprivileged, completely demonized and rerouted in contemporary liberal life. Hostility to masculinity, certainly as defined, say, before 1950 is very considerable, and it's had a very corrosive effect ideologically, aesthetically. Men can have their own pleasures in various zones, which are sort of sneered at and disprivileged. But the centrality of the heroic as a myth for life has largely gone.

The way to explicate something like Howard, as I did with Lovecraft before, is to maybe to concentrate on one of their stories. With H. P. Lovecraft I chose "The Dunwich Horror," and with Howard I would choose "Rogues in the House," which was published in *Weird Tales* in the early '30s. One fantasy critic has called it the greatest fantasy story of the 20th century, but that's just one individual's opinion. It's relatively early in the Conan series.

Conan is a northern barbarian, and because everything's fused together in Howard, he's got slightly Nordic, Germanic, and slightly Celtic traits. He's an outsider, but he has a clean code of masculine barbarism. Civilization is always seen as slightly weak-kneed and sybaritic to Howard. And yet at the same time, barbarism has its own inner order.

Now, there are counterfactual and countercultural elements

there that will be used by social anthropologists in a totally different context, like Lévi-Strauss and others, in the middle of the 20th century, but Howard means it in a different way.

There's a Left-wing streak to Howard, as there was to London, a siding with the outsider, with those ruined by capitalism, with tramps. London's book about the East End is one of the most extraordinary books about mass poverty before George Orwell's *Down and Out in Paris and London* and "How the Poor Die," which were quite extraordinary works. A poor little hospital in Paris before any sort of socialized medicine, where those who were in the bottom 10%, their corpses were just *thrown on the ground!* And they died in agony, and they kick you away and put another one on top. This is how the poor died! And Orwell said to this chap in this hospital, "But look at the state they're in!" And he said, "Well, they gave up slavery. Here's another batch." This was the attitude then. This is why things like the labor movement, even in the United States in an attenuated way, were created, to correct that imbalance as it's seen from the bottom.

The far Right, of course, always wanted not the class war of the contemporary Left, but to socialize mass life in a way that preserved the traditions of the civilization of which we're a part, that brought on what was excellent about the past and yet realized that the 50% of people who own no capital, the 50% of people who are largely excluded from all center-Right parties' definition of patriotism, are part of the country, are part of the nation, fight the country's wars for the most part when they're asked to do so, and therefore have to be within the remit of social consideration in relation to education, health, and other matters.

My explanation for Howard's support of the New Deal and that type of politics largely is along those sorts of lines. It's the sort of apolitical chap who likes country and western in a Midwestern state and supports socialized medicine up to a point, as long as it's not too costly, doesn't like Obama, and supports our troops, you see. But it's in a sort of apolitical zone which has got no real knowledge above that. Some of the instincts are right, but the ideological formulation in which that takes place is likely wrong, because even these wars—do you think Iraq was fought for ordinary white Americans? Do you think Afghanistan has anything to do with ordinary families living in Nebraska or Nevada or Kansas? None of these wars have anything to do with them at all. Even the Black Muslims have worked out that white gentiles largely are second-class citizens now in the society that they created. But that's another story, and I'd just like to concentrate on Howard.

This particular story concerns Conan from the outside, Conan as perceived by an aristocrat and fop called Murilo. Howard's a little bit of a Nordicist. He thinks southern Europeans are a bit foppish in comparison to northern Europeans. There's a streak of this. And some of the society seems to be Italy, Corinth, Zamora, but they're not. But they seem to be Italy.

Well, there's this Italian city-state that's run by a corrupt priest called Nabonidus, who's known as the Red Priest. These myths are set, these stories, mythologically encoded, are set before the beginning of recorded history and after the sinking of Atlantis, possibly a fantasy itself. So he sets them far back enough that he can do whatever he wants with them, but at the same time he can import a large amount of retrospective historical insight.

The interesting thing is the Machiavellianism of the politics of these stories. All of these societies are run extremely ruthlessly and they are run completely for the power interests of the people in charge. The nationalities don't really matter, but they are, if the gloves are off, as marauding and vengeful as their own leaders who they represent at a lower level. Truly Howard believes, with the Roman dictator Sulla, that when the weapons are out, the laws fall silent.

Now, Murilo is a courtier, a relatively corrupt courtier, in this city-state, and Nabonidus comes to him one day at a royal council meeting and gives him a small casket that contains a severed ear. And this is a warning, as it would be if a Renaissance prince in post-medieval Italy gave it to a rival, and it's: "Clear off. Get out of the city-state as quickly as possible. I'm giving you one day."

And Murilo wonders what he's going to do. He can flee, but

he's not a coward, why should he leave his own city? And in any case he's got lots of rackets on the go, you know, so he wants an out, and he thinks, "I need to assassinate Nabonidus," who runs the drunken King as a sort of priest/philosopher-king/leader of a native death cult within the city like a puppet master controls his doll.

So he needs a vassal, and he finds it in the prisons of the city where a young, heathen, northern barbarian has been captured and laid there in chains after various escapades and thefts, and this is a young man of 19 called Conan, who's twice the size of a normal man. All Howard's heroes are physically enormous, and all incredibly violent, although they all have an honor code of their own which is interesting, particularly towards the end of the story, what you might call an innate code of masculine morality and honor which is part and parcel of natural law.

The social Darwinian view that was spread throughout mass culture, particularly these types of fictions in the late 19th and early 20th centuries, is not entirely true. As all prisons and all armies testify, there's a code of honor and morality even in very extreme male behavior. Rapists are always amongst the most disprivileged in any prison. Men who attack and feed on women, for example, in very all-male and male-concentric cultural spaces are always disprivileged, always disliked, and that's because of innate feelings about how – in a very traditionalist way, what we call partly a sexist way now – men should treat women. And these things predate all modern ideas and are partly innate. And in some ways, because Howard is such an instinctualist, he brings these sorts of forces to the fore.

Now, Nabonidus wants Murilo to leave the city. Murilo hires Conan to murder Nabonidus. Conan is in his cell sucking some beef off a bone. And besides, Nabonidus is an upper-class priest, so why not murder him for money? He's an adventurer. So he decides to go with Murilo on this plot.

As always with Howard, a synopsis never does justice to the sort of the lucid dreaming of the story itself. Howard always said that he was there and that Conan was next to him like an old soldier dictating his stories, some of which will be tall stories as well.

Now, Murilo then hears that Conan has been captured because the guard that he bribed to get him out of the prison has been arrested on another offense. Conan's actually escaped in another way and joins Murilo later. Murilo, desperate, a Borgia without any sort of a family fortune, decides to murder Nabonidus himself, so he creeps up to his fortified estate, which is on the edge of town, described in this Gothic way — it's dark, it's sepulchral, it's moonlit, there's an enormous dog that roams the grounds.

Remember Conan Doyle's stories? There's always this enormous mastiff that the villain has that roams the grounds to bring people down, and that Watson shoots on Holmes' behalf usually at the end. In "The Hound of the Baskervilles," which is extraordinarily amusing because the hound is covered with phosphorous to make it glow in the dark when it races after some poor chap who's looking back, terrified, on a sort of West Country moor. And yet phosphorous is so poisonous that, the dog licks itself all the time, one lick and it's dead. But these stories are metaphorical. They're extreme exercises in the imagination. They're not concerned with these pettifogging details of which critics make too much.

Now, Murilo creeps into the garden and, horror of horrors, what does he find? He finds the dead body of the dog, and it looks as though it's been savagely mauled in a way by something he doesn't understand, by some weird thing or ape or monster. He then proceeds into the house and finds much of it wrecked. Nabonidus is nowhere to be seen, and one of his servants, Joka, has been murdered.

Suddenly he gets into the inner chamber of Nabonidus' villa, which is modeled on a Renaissance palace essentially, and he sees the Red Priest — so named because he wears this red cowl — sitting on a throne, made of alabaster, and everything's heavy and ornamental, a bit like those Cecil B. DeMille films from the '30s, everything extraordinarily overdone and luxuriant. And he creeps up to Nabonidus to stab him, and the figure turns, and it's a were-thing, or a monster of one's imagination. It's not human at all, simian rather than human. And Murilo faints, and then the story closes.

This story's in three acts. Traditionally, like a lot of Western drama, like Dante's *Inferno, Purgatory, Paradise*, you've got this three-pronged triadic element, the thesis, the antithesis, the synthesis at the end. So that's the first part.

The second part is Murilo awakens in dungeons or interconnected corridors underneath Nabonidus' house, manse, mansion. He crawls along a corridor and somebody hisses, and it's Conan. He's come into the house to murder Nabonidus because Murilo's going to pay him, and because he's a member of a cult that he dislikes and so on. Murilo scents his hair, like the young aristocrats of his era, and Conan's senses are so acute that he detects that with his nostrils, and that's the reason he doesn't attack him in the darkness.

They both decide to swear loyalty to each other. Don't forget this is an oral culture where bonds and legal sanctions are expressed orally. Howard despised the element of modern life where people say anything they want just to get their own way at any particular time. In pre-modern, say Nordic societies, the oath or something which is given verbally with strength is as binding as any legal document ever could be, even more so.

Conan and Murilo proceed looking for Nabonidus. They come out into the body of the house, which as I said resembles just sort of Renaissance, Florentine palace, and they see Nabonidus stripped, semi-naked and wounded, in a neighboring corridor, and they wonder what has replaced him up inside the house.

And what has happened, as he in a dazed way explains once he returns to full consciousness, is that his servant, who's this ape that he's taken from one of the outlying countries in Howard's imaginary kingdoms, has supplanted him as the master in the house. Howard, to a moderate degree, believed in science, believed in evolution. It was very much almost a cult then, as was eugenics. And Thak as he's called, this ape-man who wears the red because he's supplanted the human he wanted to supplant, has thrown his master, Nabonidus, into the pit and has seized control of the house. Thak sits, waiting for them to come out of the pit, because there's a bell underneath in the pits that they've crossed, a trap basically, and he knows humans are down there, and he's waiting for them.

Nationalists emerge. There's an interesting political element here, because Nabonidus is a very corrupt ruler and has the King in his thrall, so nationalists of the city-state—you could be a nationalist and of a city-state because it was the unit of civilization essentially, and a country would be city-states federated together—attempt to assassinate Nabonidus in a way that Murilo wanted to. Thak deals with them. The story fast-forwards in a very filmic way, because Howard is a visualizer. The male brain is visual and always thinks in images. And these sorts of stories are extraordinarily cinematographical in their nature and their forward, pumping lucidity.

Thak senses that they've come up from under the ground, and there are interesting pseudo-scientific elements. The Red Priest, Nabonidus is a scientist and a mage and a magician combined. It's *Religion and the Decline of Magic* in some ways, if you view it academically. He has this construction of mirrors whereby from one room you can reflect light through tubes that contain small mirrors, and it ends up being able to look into another room, so you can actually look round corners. And they can see Thak, and he can see them.

Because he needs to dispose of the bodies of the nationalists who've come into the house, Thak disappears for a time, and Conan and the others seize their chance, and they go up. Nabonidus becomes terrified when all the doors are locked, and he can't find the weapons they need to fight against his servant who's turned against him.

In the end, Conan has to face off against Thak in this quite extraordinarily violent scene. Howard was one of the most brilliant writers of physical force and conflict between men in the 20th century. There's little doubt about that. It's so immediate, you're almost there, and it is essentially visual. Conan and Thak have this clash-of-the-gods-type of titanic duel with each other, much like a scene from Homer, basically: Hector before the walls of Troy. Thak is done down in the end, and Conan, half-dead, is saluted by Murilo.

Nabonidus then tries to betray both of them, and Conan does for him, really, with a stool. He whips up a stool and throws it into his head, and he falls, and all Conan can say is, "His blood is red, not black," because in the slums of the city they said the Red Priest's blood was black because his heart was black, and Conan's a barbarian and a literalist, you see. "His blood isn't black."

There's an interesting moment when Conan is helped by Murilo because he's so hurt and wounded in the fight with Thak, and Conan pushes Murilo aside and says, "A man walks alone. When you can't stand up it's time to perish." That's not an attitude you heard from the Blair government too often, is it? These are pre-modern attitudes, you see. As somebody on Radio 4 would say now, "But that's a dangerously exclusionist notion. What about the ill, what about the weak?" And of course in that type of barbaric morality, the strong look after the weak, but only in an assent of being and natural law which is codified on the basis of the morality of strength. That's what those sorts of civilizations thought and felt.

And the other interesting thing is that he looks down on Thak, this sort-of-beast/sort-of-man that he's killed, and he says, "I didn't kill a beast tonight, but a man! And my women will sing of him."

There are two cultural views of these sorts of things. One is to regard them as remarkable pieces of creative imagination. There is other is to sort of laugh and sneer at them, and think that they represent old-fashioned values that we've thankfully gotten rid of, or moved away from.

The stories, with the exception of the Kane stories, are all pre-Christian in the most radical of terms, and yet pre-liberal and liberal/secular, which of course in the modern West is what's replaced Christianity. I would say that contemporary Catholicism is rather like the Protestantism of yesteryear, and Protestantism has become liberalism, and liberalism has morphed, strangely, without the Protestantism that gave it a moral compass, into a form of cultural Marxism, and that's what we have now.

And yet Howard's stories are very, very interesting and very dynamic and very much appeal to an imaginative element in certainly a lot of men. The belief in self-definition, the belief in the heroic as a model for life, the belief in strength but with an honor code that saves it from wanton exercise in strength without purpose, and the belief that one is part of even a tribe or a community.

In the stories, Conan's a Cimmerian. He's from a northern group. He's only got one name. He's so primal, he doesn't have any other names. Conan. Like Heathcliff in *Wuthering Heights*, he only had one name. *Heathcliff*, he doesn't need any other names. He's just a force, you see? A force of the female imagination, which is what he is. And in a strange way, the way in which he's described in that novel by Emily Brontë is very similar to the way Conan's described, but Conan's a bit more beefed out, a bit more muscular.

Many films have been made; many TV series have been made; there's a Conan industry in the 20th century. What Howard would have thought of all that no one knows. He's there, possibly on a slightly lower tier, but with Tarzan and Doctor Who and James Bond and these other iconic sort of mass popular fantasy figures. Yet in all of them, certainly in this sort of material, there's a truth to experience, there's a vividness, there's a cinematographical and representational reality, and there's a concern with courage, masculinity, and the heroic which is lacking from most areas of society, and there's also an honor code, a primitive morality if you like, which goes with it and gives it efficacy and purpose.

The other thing which differentiates this type of literature is respect for the enemy. When Terre'Blanche was murdered, I noticed liberals on the BBC giggling and sort of laughing and thinking it was all a jolly joke. These are people who are against the death penalty and believe that murder's a terrible infraction against human rights, jurisprudence, and all the rest of it. But the sort of cultural space that this work comes out of respects the enemy. Kills the enemy, respects the enemy, which of course is a soldier's emotion.

Many who've fought in wars don't disrespect the enemy. They know what they're like. British soldiers who've fought in the Falklands, American soldiers who've fought against Islamist militants, and even some of the militants themselves when they've fought against Western warriors, understand the code of the soldier and the code of the warrior on the other side. But many of these men are, spiritually, fundamentally similar men in a way, born in other groups.

Men will always fight with each other, and they're biologically prone to do so. How, in an era of mass weapons of destructive warfare, some existing and others not, that is to be worked through. It is a part of the destiny of the relationship between groups and states. But the hard-wiring that makes men competitive and egotistical and conflict-oriented is ineradicable and irreducible. And modern liberal societies which are based upon the idea of inclusionist love without thought of conflict are sentimental to the point that they will fall apart, bedeviled by their endless contradictions.

And I personally think that if you inculcate yourself, with a bit of irony and estrangement, from some of the elements of the culture of the heroic that certainly subsisted as mainstream cultural fare in our society before 1950, you have a different attitude towards what spews out of the telly every evening, and you have a different attitude towards the sort of culture that you're living in, and you have a different attitude towards great figures in your own group—and even in others—and you have a different attitude towards yourself and the future.

I give you Robert Ervin Howard, 1906 to 1936, a man who walked alone but spoke for an element, not just of America, but of what it is to be white, male, Western, and free.

Thank you very much!

Counter-Currents/*North American New Right*
June 11, 2013

Conan the Barbarian

This review will examine the work of Robert E. Howard and, in particular, his greatest creation the barbarian Conan. For the purposes of concentration and illustration, I will look at the comic strip *Zukala's Daughter*, scripted by Roy Thomas, and featuring in the 1972 Fleetway annual in Britain. It happened to be one of the earliest numbered editions of the color comic known as *Conan the Barbarian*.

Conan happens to be the superman (or Super-barbarian, in Fritz Leiber's wiles) into which Robert Ervin Howard projected fantasies of undying masculinity, the heroic, adventure without end, heterosexuality, and a sublimated racial mystique. In this story a young and precocious Conan—drawn in a mannerist and Art Deco style—meshes neatly with one of the author's poems about Zukala. Robert E. Howard was a prolific poet, and his *Selected Poems* are available on Lulu.com (the electronic publishing website).

In the piece known as *Zukala's Daughter* (based on the poem "Zukala's Hour") the plot can be briefly summarized. To my mind, it is supremely well-done—being positively filmic in its crisp and sequential execution. Conan arrives in a village on market day and discusses the price of a sword with a sword-seller. He does not have the money necessary for it, however.

Suddenly a panic or general alarm spreads among the stall-holders. This is the day—of all days—when they should have shut up shop earlier. It is the moment when the Wizard, Zukala, who dominates the town, sends an emissary to obtain tribute—a form of taxation, in other words.

A creature forms out of dots in the atmosphere and then springs into life as a tigress. It smashes the market stalls and corners a child that's become separated from its mother. Ever heroic, Conan defends the child by drawing his sword and challenging the magical tigress. It breaks his blade easily by leaping across him, and then the two of them wrestle in the dirt.

During their bout a voice in the tigress (a woman's voice) talks to him and says, "I shall never harm you—not now; not ever." Conan is bemused and attracted by the voice . . . and calls out for the tigress to return to him as it retreats from the village. The villagers gather around their champion, an uncouth barbarian from the North, and tell him the truth about the tax and its collector.

The latter is, in reality, a shape-shifting creature who, at this very moment, shall morph back into the body and soul of a woman called Zephra (the West wind). She happens to be the old magician's daughter, but the villagers regard her as a sad individual because she has the gift of second sight and can predict the moment of her own death. Both she and her father, the wizard Zukala, are apparently ageless as well—the centuries mean nothing to them.

One of the old women in the village, who remembers Zephra playing 'neath the moon when she was a child, calls out curses upon them. "I am old and wizened," she declares, "where's the fairness in that? Death to 'em, I says!"

Conan learns that the villagers are prepared to pay him 20,000 gold pieces—the price of their tax burden—if the young Barbarian will kill Zukala for them. Conan accepts with alacrity—although he may just ask the mage to leave. The swordsmith provides Conan with a new version of his old blade—the one which he eyed earlier on at the market stall. Once Conan is out of earshot, the villagers begin to plot his demise, "if and when the stripling can kill Zukala."

Conan then gains egress to the magician's castle by climbing a very tall tree and leaping across the battlements. He enters a chamber where Zukala is performing Ritual or High magic. But before this Zephra has returned home to her father—who stands waiting for her inside the battlements. "Why are you trembling like a leaf or a calf-sick mortal?" he demands of her. She then faints in his arms under the abjuration "Tell me!"

Meanwhile, Conan observes Zukala making magic and summoning up an enormous da(e)mon from Hades in the form of Jaggta-Noga. This is an interesting hybrid which consists of a centaur and a devil, in that the creature concerned is half-horse. Zukala insists that the townsfolk yonder must pay him homage, and Jaggta-Noga is dispatched to see that they do so. He will return later in this adventure with 20,000 gold pieces in the requisite sack.

Conan steals behind a rug on one of the walls only to run into Zephra — the magician's tiger-daughter. She promptly starts to make love to Conan as she has precognition or the gift of second sight . . . and she sees no reason not to get on with things! Conan is nonplussed by this, but more than keen enough to engage in passionate embraces with a sultry lovely.

Zukala, her father, then begins to materialize behind Conan. "Crom's Devils!" explodes Conan in a rare moment of humor, "do doors have no meaning in this place?" Zukala and Conan then start fighting — with Zephra trying to intercede between them. Conan's animal agility, strength, and daring — his barbarism *tout court* — outfoxes Zukala, who is used to cowering enemies like the villagers down below.

During the course of their battle, Conan cuts off half his facemask with the sword from the village seller; it reduces Zukala's power by fifty percent. Just as it looks as if it's all up with Zukala, Jaggta-Noga reappears from a window, and he and Conan start a fight to the death. The demon has brought with him the tribute which amounted to 20,000 gold pieces.

Zephra — keen to protect her lover — leaps across Conan as the tigress. But Jaggta-Noga picks her up and hurls her into the ground. She remains there lifeless and still, but recovers later. Jaggta-Noga is oblivious to the Mage's emotion over his daughter. "Let her perish, wizard. She is nothing. It is not life you should worship — but death. For even life that spans the centuries is naught to Jaggta-Noga."

Enraged by this — and anxious for his daughter — Zukala sends the demon back, back to the pit which spawned him. He then takes up his daughter, who is beginning to recover, but who keeps repeating "Conan; Conan . . ." He tells the barbarian to beware as they disappear into the ether . . . and blames him for the fact that the Barbarian has stolen his daughter's heart from him. Conan stoops to pick up the gold pieces. His mission is accomplished — the Wizard has vanished . . . what purpose is served by going back to the village . . . none at all. *The Story Ends*.

I would contend that this pastiche of a Howard poem — itself part of a longer cycle — tells you everything you need to know about Howard's fiction. We begin with the exhilaration, the sense of excitement, the existence of a Caucasian Superman, as well as the headlong action and narrative drive. The agelessness of the protagonists and the almost pulpish heterosexuality are very much in evidence.

Likewise, magic is considered to be a normal part of life and, in this sword and sorcery universe, it is the equivalent of scientific writ in our own time. It is fascinating to think that Zukala's version of Crowley or Louis Adolphe Constant is treated like the second law of Newtonian mechanics in this universe.

Broadly speaking, the moral cleanness of the barbaric character (Conan) in comparison to the civilized ones is also clearly pointed out. Indeed, one could say that all of Robert E. Howard's barbaric heroes — Bran Mak Morn, Kull, and Solomon Kane — all build up into the one Super-character, Conan; a man whose saga was left evident yet uncompleted on Howard's death.

I think the basic point of the Conan stories — and of Howard in general — is as a moral corrective. For those who feel broken, lonely, afraid, cowardly, uncombative (and so on), the Howard *mythos* in its 16 or so volumes is a wilful counterpart. Morally, his entire *mythos* is a species of counter-culture or current.

"Conan the Barbarian and Robert E. Howard"
Counter-Currents/ *North American New Right*
July 15, 2011

"Rogues in the House"

In this essay I shall seek to pick out a few themes from Robert E. Howard's writing life, using one of his most emblematic stories, "Rogues in the House," as a living illustration.

Howard certainly had (or imagined that he did) strong Irish roots which influenced much of his fiction in a Celtic direction. One only has to look at the nature of the Nemedian chronicles in the Conan *mythos* to see this. Not to mention his ever-present fascination with the Picts. This savage and ancient Scottish people are a recurrent motif throughout his career, ending with the Conan *mythos*, and best typified by his early Pictish king, Bran Mak Morn. One presumes, amongst other things, that Conan's name is abstracted from the same name in Sir Arthur Conan Doyle's august nomenclature. Conan Doyle, the world famous creator of Sherlock Holmes, had Irish roots via his Scottish ancestry.

This Hibernian influence aside, however, one of the things that always strikes one about Howard is the extreme violence of his stories—something which led them to be viewed with "disgust" by August Derleth, for example. Certainly the blood and thunder has a transgressive edge which seeks to outdo similar turbulence in the work of Frank Norris or Jack London. Nonetheless, whether or not this streak of exhibitionistic sadism has anything to do with being bullied at school and as a young man and seeking compensation, has to remain a lost biographical insight. There is definitely no ideological element to the blood-'n'-guts, unlike Norris, who in works like *Greed* (later filmed by Stroheim) luxuriates in the pitilessness of life along themes which are clearly sociobiological and Darwinian.

Another Howard trope which emerges early on is a depressive view of civilization and a related and oft expressed view about the sincerity of barbarism. He either believes in decline *à la* Spengler, or at the very least he has major problems with modernity. This comes to a head in his ready dismissal of the oil boom or black gold rush that typified Cross Plains, the Texas town where he grew up and spent most of his life.

One can see this most clearly in the treatment of Akivasha, the Stygian vampire who never died, in the latter stages of Howard's only Conan novel, *Conan the Conqueror* (otherwise known as *The Hour of the Dragon*). He contrasts the romantic legend about her, sung by students and lovers, to reality and says that it was ever thus. Reality never lives up to mankind's dreams. This depressive coda indicates that Howard had a pessimistic, mordant, and culturally conservative view of change and progress—whatever his actual political and socio-economic views.

A distrust in grand theory is also seen in his galaxy of unintellectual (but not unintelligent) heroes. These number—amongst many others—Bran Mak Morn, Solomon Kane, King Kull, Conan, and a diverse spread of boxers and cowboys. There is a certain quotidian pessimism (always morphological and culturally conservative) in having characters, who by virtue of some of their limitations, can only fight their way out of a situation.

All of these more generic themes come together in a highly illustrative Conan story such as "Rogues in the House" —a story which has been described as one of the best fantasies written in the 20th century.

One dead, One fled, One sleeping in a golden bed. —Old Rime

Rogues in the House is a revenge tragedy featuring the young nobleman Murilo who is warned to leave a walled city by the Red Priest, Nabonidus. The warning takes the form of a severed ear in a box which he gives to the young pretender at a royal banquet. Murilo realizes that it is either him or the priest—and fashions a scheme whereby he can rid himself of his nemesis.

This involves using the services of a barbaric outlander, Conan, who is a notorious thief and reaver. Murilo arranges for his escape from prison, and (after some preliminaries which do not concern us) Murilo follows his bravo into the very citadel of the Red Priest. In doing so, he almost trips over the body of an enormous hound or mastiff which haunted the expansive gardens of the mansion . . . the beast has been savagely killed.

On entering the House, he sees the Red Priest sitting in his ornamental vestments or robes. On confronting him and forcing him to turn, he discovers that the wizard has become a were-thing, assuming a ghastly alternative shape.

Murilo then awakens in some vaulted dungeons or tunnels underneath the House—where he is met by Conan, who, on gaining entry through the sewers, brought down a great grill after him that sealed up the entrance. It transpires that Nabonidus, the Red Priest, has also been thrown down into this labyrinth beneath the house.

All three men have a common nemesis now, and this is Thak, a man-ape from the East, whom Nabonidus had hitherto used as a servant. But the simian clearly had ideas above his station. On a recent evening, he appeared to go mad, but it was, in reality, a clever plot to take control of the Red Priest's house and grounds, and replace him. This involved killing Jokar, the master's taciturn other servant, a human being, as well as by sitting next to the entrance to the pits—thence to blast his enemies when they emerge from the Pits through the use of a secret chamber.

Yet other enemies, or rogues in the house, are abroad this night. These are a circle of young, ardent nationalists who seek the usurpation of the Red Priest for patriotic reasons. They steal into the mansion—fancying it unguarded—only to be blasted to Hell by Thak using the weapons of a secret chamber.

Intricate grooves fashion glass walls, within which the blossoms of the gray lotus are released. These narcotics bring madness and death. After the auto-mutilation of those in the concealed chamber, Thak opens the far glass door and allows the noxious gases to escape. He then proceeds to take the bodies to acid pits elsewhere in the house.

Seizing their chance, Conan and his companions mount the stair. But all of the doors in various vestibules are locked, and even Nabonidus, the Red Priest, is thrown into a funk by Thak. The simian soon returns, and the three collaborators hatch a plot whereby Murilo shows himself and runs away, Thak follows, and then the Barbarian lands square on his shoulders from directly above. He sinks a sharp poniard or dagger again and again into the man-ape's thews and upper body, but to no avail, until, the beast is stunned by Murilo hurling a stool, and Conan's blade finds the beast's heart. After a protracted shuddering the ape-man dies, and the voice of pathos or Howard's cultural pessimism then intrudes: "I have killed a man tonight not a beast," interpolates Conan, "and my women shall sing of him."

The plot then resolves itself in an attempt by Nabonidus to double-cross his new allies, but Conan's mind, hand, and eye coordination is too swift for him. "His blood was red, after all," mouths Conan at the end of the adventure.

In this story we can see all of Howard's many tenets on display—heroism, extreme masculinity, violent heroics, a spellbinding plot, and sense of adventure. It is all combined with a cultural shadow: the anti-progressivism, mordant wit, and distrust of civilization which may well have folded into his own suicide, aged 30, in 1936.

Robert E. Howard's "Rogues in the House"
Counter-Currents/*North American New Right*
August 25, 2011

THE HOUR OF THE DRAGON
(CONAN THE CONQUEROR)

PART 1

Moving on from my recent review of Robert E. Howard's "Rogues in the House," I would like to have a look at the only full-length Conan novel, *The Hour of the Dragon* (sometimes known as *Conan the Conqueror*).

This piece again illustrates the subliminal racialism of the Howard *mythos* as well as providing a template for his mordant, pessimistic, and ultra-conservative views about civilization. Both tendencies are strongly in evidence in *The Hour of the Dragon*.

In this novel Conan has been reigning for a while as the king of Aquilonia, but trouble is brewing in the neighboring kingdom of Nemedia. The plot revolves around the reincarnation of a 3,000-year-old magician, Xaltotun of Python in Acheron, in order for him to safeguard the stolen Heart of Ahriman and bring to power a circle of conspirators in both Nemedia and Aquilonia.

The elderly Nemedian king—friendly to Conan—dies in an infernal plague, brought into being by the magician, and one of the plotters known as Tarascus replaces him on the Nemedian throne. All peace treaties are then abrogated with neighboring Aquilonia, and both powers prepare for war. The Nemedians burn a village, cross the border under Tarascus, and then encamp awaiting the Aquilonian host.

Conan has disturbed dreams the night before the battle. As a result of the black sorcery of Xaltotun, he is visited by a waif of the night, a child of the outermost gulf. The icy hand of this skeletal figure pins him to a fur dais in his regal tent, and he has to sit out the battle, another wearing his harness in front of the Aquilonian host.

At a key point in the battle, hypnotic suggestion is used to tempt the lesser man in Conan's harness over the river with the cream of his Kingdom's knights. They are trapped in a defile behind the Nemedian lines, which crashes down to earth via magical intervention, killing Conan's lookalike and leaving the army leaderless. It then breaks, as defenseless as spume before the storm. The Devil's own sorcery rides and fights for Nemedia. Conan, bereft in his kingly tent, staggers out to do battle with Tarascus, but his life is spared by Xaltotun.

This section leads to the part of the plot which really concerns us. Xaltotun arrives in his chariot, drawn by black stallions who never seem to tire, and he throws a magic bauble at Conan. He knocks it aside contemptuously. This sets off an explosion which fells him to the ground. He is then put in Xaltotun's chariot and carried back to the Nemedian palace in the capital, Belverus. Xaltotun spares Conan to use as a pawn in future power plays with his allies — such as Tarascus and Valerius — and has his body loaded with chains and placed in his private chamber.

Conan soon revives and realizes that the reincarnated black magician is the real power behind the conspirators against whom he is arrayed. Finally, after an inconclusive interview in which he refuses to become a vassal, Conan is carried down into the Pits beneath the castle. The guardians of the pits are four enormous black men — whether servants of Xaltotun or Tarascus is never made clear. One of them racially abuses Conan as he lies in chains in his cell — but he soon learns the error of his ways, since Conan breaks his head open by pulling his slack chains taut, using them as a devastating weapon. His companions carry the brained African away on silent feet, leaving Conan alone to the tender mercies of the Pits.

Riding hard, Tarascus reaches Belverus with a small retinue after the battle, determined to act against the black magician who holds them all in thrall. First, he steals the Heart of Ahriman — a flaming magical jewel which restored the magician to life — and second, he goes down into the Pits, secretly approaches Conan's door from the other side, and unlocks it. This means that he is vulnerable to some nemesis from without who can only make his way to him from further inside the Pits.

After a while a love interest supervenes, and the slave-girl

Zenobia, who has long been in love with Conan from a distance, releases him from his chains in the darkness. She has stolen the keys from the black guards who sleep from some drugged wine she has given them. Conan is immediately suspicious of her advances, but appreciates the fact that he is now free and able to smite his enemies with a 15-inch poniard (a dagger) which the girl provides him.

Zenobia offers to meet him at the entrance to the Pits ahead of a flight of stairs spiraling upwards—but, first of all, he will have to brave the Pits and anything which Tarascus may have unleashed to finish off the barbarian king once and for all. After having traversed half of their extent, Conan's acute senses realize that he is being followed by a silent man-eater. Reminiscent of Thak in "Rogues in the House," this is an ape from Vilayet which stalks human prey, remains silent throughout, and breaks open the bones for the marrow they contain.

Conan rolls himself into a ball, and poniard first, leaps between the ape's outstretched hands and marker-claws. He does this in order to reach the creature's great pulsating chest, where the heart is underneath two pronounced shields. He successfully finds what he is looking for, stabs through it with the poniard, and leaps clear, while trusting his innate strength to save him from being dismembered by the convulsive grappling of the gray Ape.

In these and other passages, Howard skilfully compiles a series of vignettes into a novel-length narrative. One also detects the Beowulf-like heroics in such a story. Moreover, unlike most post-'60s cultural fare of a similar sort, there is an ever-present racial element to this heroic idealism. It cannot really be brooked or denied; it exists, rather in the manner of Elizabethan tragedy, as a skull beneath the skin.

Counter-Currents/*North American New Right*
September 1, 2011

PART 2

In my previous installment, I had brought Conan up from

the pits underneath the Royal palace at Belverus in Nemedia. He was in the company of Zenobia, the slave-girl who had helped to rescue him from the pits, before Tarascus' marrow-eating monkey would have burst into his cell and discovered him defenseless. Together they journey through secret passages in the castle before Conan becomes apprised of a hated voice.

This is Tarascus, King of Nemedia at Almaric's bidding, who is addressing a thief in a private chamber over the disposal of the Heart of Ahriman. (This was the great flaming jewel which had resuscitated Xaltotun, the magician of Python, back to life.) Tarascus enjoins the fellow to take a boat from a neighboring country and cast the jewel into the sea. The thief departs, pulling a slouch hat over his features, and Conan launches an attack on Tarascus which is reminiscent of a wounded tiger. He misses his footing at the crucial moment, however, and the poniard tears down the King's ribs rather than through his heart — the blow is not mortal.

Having raised a hornets' nest, Conan retreats to another chamber with Zenobia, kisses her passionately, and then rips some gold bars from the window — prior to making his escape through the gardens. He eventually discovers a sturdy horse which she had tethered at a nearby fountain and makes his way to the Aquilonian border.

The situation at the border is quiet, only stragglers are left, and, in the armor of a slain mercenary, most people give Conan a wide berth. He does discover some Nemedian rabble attempting to hang an old woman from a bramble — she turns out to be a witch called Zelata, who befriends the King, and shows him a vision of Aquilonia's parlous state.

This section enables Howard to dwell disdainfully on civilization and his belief in its insubstantial or skin-deep quality. For example, immediately after Conan's alleged death, the mob took over in the Aquilonian capital, Tarantia, and wouldn't listen to reason. The barons distrusted each other and few would ride with the small band of Poitainians who had come up from the south to sustain the King's cause.

Conan had no son and heir, he was only a lone adventurer, and men's memories are fickle and short — this is what Howard seems to be saying. Many men were prepared to bend the knee to Valerius — even if they privately sensed that his rule might be sadistic and disastrous, purely because he had the blood of the old dynasty in his veins. Such, in Howard's opinion, is the folly and venality of men: they choose the worse option having made a spectacle of the best. (For, although something of a New Deal democrat in his own inclinations, Howard is a metaphysical pessimist about human nature in general and governmental institutions in particular.)

Conan is startled by these revelations, but he soon rediscovers his poise and begins to plot the reconquest of his Kingdom. Zelata urges him against a direct military strategy, however, and argues that first he must make safe the Heart of Ahriman — the heart of his Kingdom, the one thing which is strong enough to hold out against Xaltotun's magic. The men of Aquilonia do not fear Nemedia's pikestaffs and spears — it is the black arts of Xaltotun which causes them to pause in their tracks.

Conan then journeys into occupied Aquilonian territory and seeks out the comradeship of one of his key supporters, a patrician called Servius Galannus. He is startled and mortified to find the King alive — having heard the great bell toll his dirge in Tarantia many days before. They make their way to a secluded chamber in his mansion, and Servius imparts to Conan everything that's occurred. The treachery of certain barons is mulled over, as is the lot of the common people under Valerius. Likewise, they discuss the balance of forces on the Nemedian side — and how, unless they can match the magic of Xaltotun, there will be no rising of forces possible amongst the Aquilonians.

Conan is enraged to hear that slavery has been selectively reintroduced and learns that the countess Albiona is to be executed in the Iron Tower that very night for refusing to become Valerius' mistress. (Howard here commends Conan for not thinking like a civilized man — and for having ideas which run in irregular channels.)

The King decides to go into Tarantia and rescue Albiona that very night — even though Servius regards it as the height of folly. And, much later, disguised as a traveler, Conan enters Tarantia and makes his way to the Iron Tower—a fortress or citadel which predates the modern capital, and many of the secrets of which he knows. Having entered it by a circuitous route, Conan replaces the Nemedian executioner and reveals himself at the paroxysm of the execution. He makes off with the superlatively relieved Countess after having dispatched two masked Nemedians and a traitorous Aquilonian who informs Valerius with his dying breath that Conan still lives.

During his escape from the Iron Tower, Conan was assisted by the followers of a minority religion, Asura, whom he had befriended during the time of his kingship. One of their number had recognized the King under his traveler's garb—given that their cult looks to rend the veil or peer beneath the mask of illusion.

Deep in one of their concealed temples, Conan holds a council of war with Hadrathus (Asura's high priest) and Albiona. This confirms the reality of Xaltotun's rebirth and the fact that he has to be separated from the Heart of Ahriman to become manageable. Conan is able to tell the priest that the Heart has been stolen by Tarascus from the Acheronian wizard as he slept, and that a thief was then commanded to throw it into the sea.

Hadrathus is convulsed by the news—a Xaltotun separated from the flaming jewel is a mere half of the mage he once was. They begin to plot how they will get hold of the gem—given that Conan believes no self-respecting thief will scuttle the treasure. Instead he will sell it to a rich merchant for gold in the hand.

In all of this we see Howard's mordant wit, anti-civilizational bias, and belief in White heroics, as well as his use of fiction for masculine wish-fulfillment fantasies.

Counter-Currents/*North American New Right*
September 16, 2011

PART 3

In our synopsis and analysis, we left Conan and Hadrathus discussing how to regain the initiative by seizing the Heart of Ahriman. Conan then heads south in the funereal barge of a follower of Asura—to make sure that he and Albiona are unmolested—and he quickly makes up the leagues necessary to visit Count Trocero's province of Poitain in the deep south of Aquilonia. From there, he equips himself with a black stallion and crosses the river into Zingara looking for a merchant who has been sold the flaming gem by Tarascus' thief. The merchant in question was from Koth, and with foolhardy recklessness he had crossed into Zingara heading for the great seaport of Messantia. Conan then becomes involved in a series of adventures to return the Heart to his control for the good of Aquilonia, and the ultimate defeat of both Xaltotun and the Nemedians.

On looking for the merchant Zorathus and his strongbox, Conan discovers him in the feudal keep of a lord, Valbroso, who is just one rung up from a robber chieftain. They have heedlessly tortured the merchant to force him to open his reinforced box—and already we see that the great flaming jewel is borne aloft by mayhem and brigandage. Zorathus revenges himself on Valbroso by getting him to prick his finger on a poisoned stud on the containing box—by which time he is already dying. But the lord's lieutenant, Beloso, has been driven mad by the flaming gem, and with both captive and master dead, he seizes his chance to make off with it. He brings the box down heavily on Conan's helmeted skull and makes his escape into the ghoul-haunted woods along Argos' border with Zingara.

The sequence with Zorathus and Valbroso enables Howard to dwell on the perfidy of the human condition, its competitiveness and malevolence, the only morally competent characters being Conan and possibly Zorathus. Beloso is treacherous, Valbroso utterly Machiavellian, the Torturer bestial, and so on ... while Valbroso's clan or band are little different from wolves held together by fear of their lord and respect for his acumen.

Conan pursues the jewel-mad Beloso out of Zingara and into Argos before they finally arrive in the port city of Messantia (already mentioned). Thereupon he seeks out an old acquaintance, Publio, a rich merchant who worked his way up from a dive on the waterfront due to his dealings in the past with corsairs like Conan.

A tangled skein of plot then ensues. Publio plots Conan's death to free himself from the past; a Stygian galley containing an arch-priest settles in the city to seize the gem, and four oriental killers are set upon Conan's traces by Valerius, the new King of Aquilonia, who is determined that his rival, Conan, becomes a legend again as quickly as possible.

All of this leads the Stygian priest to murder Beloso by magic and make off with the jewel; Conan follows and is accosted by Publio's toughs led by one of his servants, Tiberio. He finishes most of them off but is finally knocked unconscious and later finds himself taken aboard an Argossean galley, which he seizes control of by engineering a slave revolt, so that he can follow the Stygian more easily.

He finally tracks the Stygian galley (with the Heart) to their port city of Khemi, and, leaving the Argossean vessel tied up in a remote estuary, he assails this Stygian city single-handedly looking for the gem. Eventually — and after many adventures — he tracks the Heart of Ahriman to a vault underneath a pyramid.

The Stygians, in Howard's estimation, are based on ancient Egypt with a religion modeled upon their Book of the Dead. The sequence beneath the pyramid enables Howard to explore the hollowness and pretension of much human myth, the reality often being much more sordid than the romantic illumination of it.

This relates, in a foursquare way, to the vampire Akivasha who lives underneath the Temple of Set, one of the great Stygian pyramids. In Conan's mythos she is worshiped by lovers and romantics as the woman who never died, but, in reality, she has traded eternal life for a blood-laced place in the shadows. Conan, a famously unintrospective hero, has a moment of awakening when he grasps the hollowness of many saving myths.

Finally, there is a great showdown between the Stygian

priests who have stolen the Heart and the pursuing Orientals acting for Valerius, Aquilonia's current King. Conan allows them to fall on each other until it falls to him to clean up the remainder. Finally, and with the help of a reincarnated Stygian magician, Conan leaves Khemi's temples with the Heart of Ahriman—the life-giving jewel which Xaltotun's magic cannot touch. He has squared the circle and now has a weapon which can beat back the influence of the once dead Pythonian magician.

Now he is in a position to return to his Kingdom and reclaim it from the usurpers Amalric, Tarascus, Valerius, and Xaltotun. The final installment will tell everyone how he manages to achieve this.

Counter-Currents/North American New Right
September 22, 2011

Part 4

In our final installment we will examine the end of this novel and its *dénouement*. The Heart of Ahriman—the foundation to resist Xaltotun's magick—has been obtained by Conan after numerous adventures. This means that the Aquilonians do not need to fear his necromancy as they begin their final rebellion against the Nemedians—prior to expelling them from the kingdom for good.

Conan begins to knit together the sinews of his army, involving the Gundermen from the north and the Bossonians from the west, together with his Poitanian allies, under Prince Trocero, from the deep south. He moves around the Southwest of Aquilonia—not giving battle to Tarascus—and appearing and disappearing, almost at will. This is designed to destabilize the Nemedians.

The latter are also put off balance by Xaltotun's growing ambition—together with his possible desire to bring back the ancient kingdom devoted to black magic known as Acheron. In the presence of the rival satraps—Amalric, Tarascus, and Valerius—he is careful to speak only of a new empire of this earth—not a resuscitation of a magical one which is 3,000 years old. Xaltotun murders the ex-priest of Mitra who brought him back to life—primarily as a punishment for his revealing too much about the arch-wizard's ultimate plans.

While Conan prepares his rebellious army for battle, Xaltotun comes to the camp of the Nemedian leaders. The blindness and cruelty of Valerius' kingship, and the beacon of light which is Conan's resurfacing, means that this is a revolt like no other. Xaltotun tells them to expect a flood which will trap the Aquilonians on either side of a river that has burst its banks. Each smaller force can then be dispatched by the Nemedian knights.

He goes to his tent in order to prepare the rain magic, but the witch Zelata and the priests of Asura, aided by the Heart of Ahriman, are acting against Xaltotun in order to frustrate his plans. They now have the power and the ability to do so. The river in question does rise in spate but only by a foot or so, and Conan is able to throw both armies across so that they unite and form one cohesive whole.

The Nemedian leaders are astounded—for the first time in their association with him the black Pythonian's magic has failed them. But they have no time to dwell on this; Conan is a real and ever-present danger. They march against him to a stronghold in the Gorelian hills—the last redoubt or battle-stage for many an Aquilonian king. Conan means to emerge victorious—defeat is unthinkable.

With things set for the battle on the morrow, a traitor comes forward from the Aquilonian camp. This is a broken mountebank or vagabond of an individual who offers to lead Valerius, the Aquilonian king, round the back of Conan's army at the high point of the battle. He is prepared to do all of this for as much gold as he can carry. But, in reality, it is a trap for Valerius set by all of the men he has ruined.

Aided by a mist from the priests of Asura, Valerius and his Aquilonian renegades are led into a defile with only one exit in a different part of the mountain range. It is no threat to Conan's lines whatsoever. Once imprisoned, the tyrant and his key mercenaries are done to death from the cliff by rock, spear, and arrow. Moreover, at the high point of the battle, Valerius' standard—a dragon upon a scarlet backdrop—is brandished by a horseman amidst Conan's lines. It is a testament to the fact that the Hour of the Dragon is over!

Xaltotun tries one last magical intervention—a piece of black thaumaturgy involving the demons of the lower earth. But he is upstaged by Zelata and Hadrathus, the high priest of Asura, both of whom have been given new confidence by their possession of the Heart of Ahriman, the heart of sorcery. At the height of his human sacrifice, Xaltotun is struck down by fire from the great jewel and is returned to the state of a mummy. "I only saw him as a mummy—never a living man!" claims Zelata sourly.

Both white magicians then give a signal to Conan's army to charge, and they do so—downhill—at breakneck speed, and in such a way as causes the Nemedian lines to be broken and smashed asunder. As the Nemedians flee the field, in a confused *mêlée*, Almaric is killed in a joust by one of Conan's generals, and finally the Nemedian king, Tarascus, is brought low by a great blow from Conan's broadsword. He surrenders and agrees to leave the Kingdom with all his forces, reversing slavery and paying a large indemnity. His body will remain in trust or forfeit until all of this is carried out.

In the uproarious scenes at the novel's close, the entire Aquilonian host declares Conan to be their king and he urges upon Tarascus the following restitution: the slave-girl, Zenobia, shall be raised from the Nemedian seraglio to be the Queen of Aquilonia.

In this analysis and synopsis we have pointed out the Caucasian heroics, hero-worship, and fantasy-mongering. But it is only fair to draw attention to a biting Spenglerian pessimism and an ultra-conservative pathos, in terms of cultural politics. For, buried at the very heart of what can appear to be pulp fiction, is a zest for life and death which transcends the *Zeitgeist* and imbues a spirit of warriorship in all who attend to it.

Counter-Currents/*North American New Right*
October 4, 2011

SOLOMON KANE

This review will look at Robert E. Howard's second most important hero to Conan the Barbarian — namely, the Puritan hero Solomon Kane. Kane could have been a more ideological hero than Conan, yet the stories themselves don't read that way.

For the purposes of analysis, I shall be looking at a curiosity that was published in 1968 by a hitherto obscure house called Peter Haddock Limited. The volume, entitled *The Hand of Kane*, bears the imprimatur of Glenn Lord, the then executor for the Howard estate, and was printed in Hungary (behind the Iron Curtain) to reduce printing costs. It consists of four stories about Solomon Kane all set in darkest Africa — a continent or template which Howard uses for dreaming and that gives free reign to his love of the supernatural.

Solomon Kane is a Puritan from the turn of the 17th century and is one of the most direct attempts in history to mine the Protestant heritage for heroic myths and motifs. The stories are slightly less developed than the Conan saga, but they are still very fine in terms of tales of action within a fantasy genre. Theologically we are never told what sect Solomon is in or was born into, so we have to presume that it was a mainstream Puritan or nonconformist current.

One of the fascinating things about Solomon Kane is the degree to which he is *not* a Christian hero. Admittedly he tends to fight for the underdog and oppressed, but his actions are closer to the paganism or stoicism of the ancient world. Christianity — for Solomon — is a highly Gentile faith where the individual battles the forces of darkness in order to lead to a redemptive outcome, and the God of his people (the English) is readily invoked.

Howard isn't particularly interested in Protestant theology — and much of the character's grimness and sobriety could be attributed to other causes. Although steeped in Calvinism, Solomon invokes the Bible relatively rarely — although at the end of the story "Wings in the Night" there is a superb passage of the Authorized Version (1611) in which the author gives full vent to a kind of literary ventriloquism. The text goes something like:

> The absence of the Lord's light upon the earth led to plunder by the forces of darkness. Men were chained, alone, friendless, and found themselves covered by a dark pall. Only when the fight is resumed against the powers of the dark can a man come who walks squarely in the ways of the Lord. Heed me! All who would enter the Kingdom must strive to free Man from his toils in order to lead a life free from the curse of those evil powers which beset him.

It all then becomes an issue of what you define—in this Manichean cosmos—as good and evil. Given that the stories are all incredibly violent and predatory—and Mankind is everywhere depicted as living in a state of Nature—it is relatively easy to compute: evil is what oppresses you.

Another interesting feature is how nearly Solomon's antics equate to power morality purely on the individual level. This veers towards the later Calvinist heresy known as Antinomianism, which is fiercely bound up with doctrines of election. In Calvinism, the elect is predetermined for salvation but knows not itself. In Antinomianism, however, the elect can become apprised of their salvation.

If the Elect knows it will be saved, what is to stop them acting in a power-moral, aristocratic, or non-dualist fashion? Very little, one supposes: this offers the intriguing spectacle of Nietzsche and Stirner being approached well over 200 years before their time. All of these permutations led to one of the greatest works of Scottish literature, James Hogg's *The Private Memoirs and Confessions of a Justified Sinner*. (This text is a remarkable example of Gothic Romanticism which was revived by André Gide in the early part of the 20th century.)

In the volume, *The Hand of Kane*, which I mentioned earlier, four stories are to be found called "The Hills of the Dead,"

"Hawk of Basti," "Wings in the Night," and "The Children of Asshur." All of them give free reign to Howard's love of the supernatural—although the incongruity of a Puritan hero using magic against darker forms of the same seems to escape Howard.

Sometimes one realizes that Solomon Kane is one of the stepping-stones towards Conan the Barbarian and his commitment to Protestantism is synthetic at best.

In the "Hills of the Dead," Kane rescues an interconnected series of villages from a plague of vampires. "'Tis a thing against Nature," he states laconically. "In my land they are called vampires. I never expected to discover an entire nation of them." In the climax of the story a great array of vultures swoop down upon the living dead-men as Kane battles a host of around 150 of the creatures. This resembles a watercolor by Frank Frazetta, as Solomon Kane swings his musket repeatedly in order to batter into smithereens the skulls of this vampire army.

In "Hawk of Basti," Kane meets a fellow white man in the jungle who uses European knowledge to dominate various tribes of Africans. Some of the period detail is interesting—particularly when the "Hawk" discusses the Tudor period with Solomon, most of whose replies are blunt and to the point. Mary Tudor harried mercilessly the folk of his faith; whereas Elizabeth proved more tolerable, but later on, promises were broken.

Behind all of this lies the inescapable reality—from Howard's perspective—that Puritan dissatisfaction with England led to the creation of early modern America. For, as Tomislav Sunić forcibly points out in *Homo americanus*, America is a Protestant fundamentalist society in which secular liberalism lodges as a necessary counterbalance.

The third story leads to Kane battling, as the Chosen savior (*sic*), a wedge of Harpies who were driven down into Africa by Jason in antiquity. This extremely bloody and sadistic tale involves an inferno at the end that delineates one of the Hellish triptychs by Hieronymus Bosch. Bosch—although orthodox Catholic—very much shares the same Apocalyptic fancies as the Protestants of later centuries.

The final tale, "Children of Asshur," deals with the fate of the Assyrians whom the Old Testament designates as the "accursed of God" because of their enslavement of the ancient Israelites.

All in all, Solomon Kane is a worthy forerunner to Conan in the unfolding Howard *mythos*—and the heroic mantle of the Puritan reaver and warrior, dressed all in black, with a lugubrious countenance, a large slouch hat, pistols, dirk, broadsword, and shot, stays long in the memory.

"Solomon Kane and Robert E. Howard"
Counter-Currents/*North American New Right*
July 25, 2011

H. P. LOVECRAFT:
ARYAN MYSTIC

"Homo homini lupus." (Man is a wolf to his kindred.)
— Plautus

Howard Phillips Lovecraft was born in Providence, Rhode Island, in 1890. His father died in 1898 in Butler Hospital, Providence, allegedly from nervous exhaustion due to overwork, but, in actuality, it was occasioned by general paresis or insanity brought on by tertiary syphilis.

Lovecraft was then raised by his mother and two aunts, Lilian and Annie Emeline Phillips. A cosseted and mollycoddled youth, he developed psychosomatic illnesses of varied kinds — most of which disappeared the further he traveled from his aunts. Did his mother go insane from what might be described as a syphilitic complication, the latter aided and abetted by arsenic tincture as a "preventative"? She also died in Butler Hospital on May the 21st, 1921.

Lovecraft's stories are divided by some into three categories: namely, the macabre, the dreamy, and the mythological. His tales all incarnate the premise of some genetic inheritance or other — usually in a morbid manner. They often illustrate notions of a guilty precognition — the former nearly always of a morphic or physiological kind. Other leitmotifs — which are almost Wagnerian in import — prove to be non-human influences, usually of a cosmic indent, that impact on mankind in a detrimental way.

Indeed, Lovecraft's view of a mechanistic and amoral universe goes well beyond Augustinian pessimism — the usual basis for Christian conservatism. It essentially looks to a benumbing terror at civilization's heart; and it also speaks of Pascal's nausea at those cold, interstellar depths. Fate plays a large role here as well, and under such a dispensation progressive notions of free will or evolution fall sheer.

Lovecraft felt that Western society was laboring under an

implicit or immediate threat. This took — somewhat inevitably — a racial form. A convinced Anglophile, Lovecraft saw miscegenation and ethnic *kaos* everywhere in contemporary America — not least in New York City during his brief marriage. His discourse tends to intuit hierarchy, to wish to manage or reify it, and then to string it uppermost like a mobile by Angus Calder. He attempts here — morphically — to create hierarchies of an exclusive or traditional kind, so as to provide Nietzsche's pathos of difference.

All of this is undertaken — without any notion of paradox — in order to make life more three-dimensional or tragic. Truly, a pessimist and an ultra-conservative who's on a par with Robert Burton's *The Anatomy of Melancholy*, Lovecraft even sees science as grist to his mill. Usually positive inquiry — or evidentialism — is thought of as liberalism's handmaiden, but, in Lovecraft's *oeuvre*, it can serve as a basis for overthrowing "Enlightenment" nostrums.

Let us take, by way of illustration, the relatively lengthy tale which is known as "The Dunwich Horror." It first appeared in the fantasy magazine *Weird Tales* in 1929. This story involves the idea of transformation or radical change — i.e., of a man into a beast and a beast-man into nothingness. At one remove from the present, a decayed family of backwoodsmen merges in with entities from the beyond. They do so on Sabbat eve up on those stones in dense undergrowth and pursuant to bringing down what exists without.

Two spawn are bequeathed to their witch-mother, Lavinia, one of whom is visible — the other less so. Initially, her father extends the homestead in order to accommodate new borders. An extension is added so as to conceal beneath its wood the threat of what grows within it. A sharp hammering was heard at night, as Old Man Whateley sought to extend his Imperium.

Gradually the more presentable of the two sons, Wilbur, begins to seek out forbidden knowledge and secrets. These tomes happen to be stored at Miskatonic University — a creation of Lovecraft's. Wilbur's deformed torso and trunk — not to mention his devil's foot — as well as his searching out of unhallowed lore, leads to suspicion.

One eminent professor, Doctor Armitage, becomes disturbed by Whateley's desire to access arcane texts. Many of these are in Latin and feature the scribblings of the Elizabethan astrologer John Dee. Bemused by Dr. Armitage's refusal, Wilbur determines to break into the library at a later date. In a Hammer horror denouement, young Whateley dies trying to extract unhallowed arcana from this "Bodelian."

Doctor Armitage — concerned at the presence of satyrs in New England — decides to investigate up country. He gathers a posse around him. Meanwhile, Wilbur's brother has burst out of the house — after the deaths of his mother and grandfather. He (Doctor Armitage) then proceeds to investigate this decayed hermitage. In a dramatic crescendo — punctuated by Lovecraft's love of Yankee patois — a final blaze takes place.

It involves the other Whateley who's observed by some New England peasants floating into the ether. (In this scene, the man's senses are blasted out of all expectation!) The first thing to note is the beast's categorization: this involves anthropomorphism. For it consists of a writhing and insensate "mass" of snakes, pipes, vessels, or tubular instruments. (These can't help resembling a cancer.) It also floats abroad without any discernible support — and yet above its tendrils, suckers and mouths (or living stoves) we see a remarkable sight. It happens to be a face — or, more accurately, a half-face which hovers above Whateley's jelly. It looks like a revolving disc. You see, this creation of inbreeding, miscegenation, Galton's dysgenics and lower occultism, is leaving the planet. He/"it" proves to be searching out the Old Ones beyond the stars — he's going back.

For Lovecraft's tale seems to be a rite of passage, in that it's a cautionary wedding of an albino's litter with the occult's left-hand. Could it be thought of as a celebration (albeit in reverse) of a Comus rout? It ticks off the absolute in order to cry out against the cosmos, somewhat pessimistically. Does it resurrect Evola's example here? Certainly, all of this causes the pot to boil over. After all, it's a medley of the albino, racial *kaos*, a search for "elementals," Satanism, unsacrosanct lore and 19th century degeneration theory *à la* Nordau...

An effluvium which contrives to alter our perspective of a

New England dreamer; a man who once produced a journal called *The Conservative*. A 'zine which was mimeographed in form and truly reactionary in spirit . . .

At this distance, we can see Howard Phillips Lovecraft more clearly: and he floats, free of clutter, like a mystic, a visionary, or a mystagogue. His imagination is on fire, and he exists amid a transport of energy. Truly, he has seen the Black Sun — to use imagery from the New Zealand writer Kerry Bolton. This former resident of Rhode Island can now be considered as an Aryan *fakir* — or a *mage* who dreams of purple in obsidian (implacably so). These nightmares exist amidst blocks of granite — whether tinted red or green — and in subdued light. He (Lovecraft) preaches the end of the discernible, even the beginning of a cosmic *kaos* — sometimes called cosmicism.

Moreover, these processes portend a notion of order; i.e., they move towards it before doubling-back or switch-blading. Most definitely, Lovecraft has drawn the Tarot card known as The Tower in either Waite's or Crowley's deck. He succeeds in preaching Apollyon (thereby). Indeed, no other fantasist reckons on such Revelations as these — in the manner of the Apocalypse or the New Testament's last reading. (A discourse which never repudiates the scientific inquiry that this astronomer believed in.)

Hail to thee, Howard Phillips Lovecraft, and your dark visions of yore. They are bound to end up in either autophagy or a triptych by Memling. Isn't it an example of a Western Gothic or baroque sensibility? Or might it be seen in terms of George Steiner's *shoah* drama, *The Portage to San Christobal of A.H.*? In this respect, could his lexicon haunt mass consciousness as Grendel's latest trip?

Counter-Currents/*North American New Right*
August 20, 2010

FRANK FRAZETTA:
THE NEW ARNO BREKER?

Frank Frazetta was an artist who created countless paintings, comics, and book and album covers with a focus on the superhero, fantasy, and science fiction genres. He lived between 1928 and 2010. This brief summation will not itemize or describe the biographical profile of his career, but attempt to elucidate themes in what his art is about.

A child prodigy, born in Brooklyn, Frazetta started to draw and paint almost as he became sentient. He was certainly engaged in original artistic creation from the age of 2 to 4, and thereafter. This is itself both interesting and provocative, in that it reveals yet again (if it were needed) that real talent for anything creative is generic, biological, somatic, genetic, as well as inheritable across the bloodlines within an extended family. There are also occasional flibbertigibbets or leaps across generations. Man, in these matters, is 80% nature and 20% nurture, with even the social or environmental factors being a subset of ecology.

One of the things which is most notable about Frank Frazetta's art is that it is intrinsically male—both conceptually, in terms of execution, and the way in which the visual consciousness responds to his configuration. Men are visualizers who, for the most part and irrespective of language skills, think in images before they communicate or turn them into words. Like Arno Breker—the German neo-classicist from the earlier part of the 20th century with whom I'm comparing him—Frazetta deals with strength, heroic cruelty, ardor, the warrior aesthetic, and even Odinic themes. The art is explicitly pagan in an unconscious sense of that term—that is, without any theory or necessary cultural overlay whatsoever.

The view of women in his work is, likewise, explicitly male and completely sexual. Unless they are sword-and-sorcery hags, witches, drones, or Erdas (earth mothers) for reasons of plot, all women in Frazetta are beautiful. But they are erotically magnificent as well. The feminist critique of Frazetta and similar populist artists (whether one speaks of Dworkin, Jong, or Millett) would be to accuse him of stereotypes, "objectification," sexualization, or soft pornography. But one has a response: these are the symbolist and icon fantasies that all heterosexual men have about women all of the time. The female (in the male gaze) is always made iconic, transfigured *per se*, and seen as an object and part-worshiped. Few men openly admit to this, but it doesn't stop it from being a reality. Frazetta happens to be relatively unusual in his completely unapologetic attitude about it.

In various forms of modernist art, of course, there is often a guilt-laden male *Angst* about the presentation of the female form. Nonetheless, the post-feminist thinker Camille Paglia can't be acceded to either, in her view that pornography is a species of art. Artistic activity (no matter how generalized in impact or effect) has to be mediated. It passes through a mind or sensibility — and is individualized thereby.

(Note: modern art is immensely complex in its heterogeneity — for example, the semi-heroic visualization of the male in Elisabeth Frink's sculptures; or the erotic worship of women in Felix Labisse's paintings — occupy a very different area.)

Now let's turn, as a companion piece to the above, to Frazetta's worship of violence and force in Men — the true kernel of his representative work. His vision of masculinity is intrinsically heroic, God-like, transfigured, heightened, and somewhat inevitably tends towards the Olympian. Despite its formulaic obviousness, it does appear that superheroes and all forms of heroic fantasy replicate, pretty much exactly, how archaic, pre-modern, and polytheist societies viewed their Gods. To adapt a cliché: Superheroes are the new Gods. Nonetheless, the fascination with male strength, preparedness, and untouchability — as an object of implacable fury — animates Frazetta's aesthetic.

In some ways, it is a working-class idiolect: by which I mean that it has not been softened by bourgeois psychologism. It remains other, doleful, brooding, chthonian, very violent . . . even anti-metaphysical.

Frazetta used to boast that he never read any of the heroic pulps — such as those by Robert E. Howard or Edgar Rice Burroughs—that he had occasion to illustrate. Yet, although probably true, this fact doesn't have any intrinsic import. What matters is that, visually speaking, he completely intuited what these prose works were about. He quite literally approached them from a different part of the brain. Indeed, his presentation of Conan the Barbarian (Howard's hero) as a primitive god, virtually the personification of his own deity Crom, is a case in point.

For Frazetta's work remains quintessentially fascistic at the level of mass culture—everyone understands this, not least its liberal opponents. Even though they might not follow every interconnecting strand in its argument—all feminists, cultural Marxists, Left-liberals, egalitarians, and progressives know what is being celebrated here. This is why, despite some of his canvases fetching over a million dollars at his death, Frazetta's work is traduced by elite taste. It happens to be liberal elite taste, mind you.

Given this, all culture which glories in the warrior male has been forced down into Hades, into the depths; into a realm of chapbooks, blogs, 'zines, rock music album covers, science fiction book covers, B-movies, and mass television, etc.... Liberal-Left critics don't look at it except to condemn it, except commercially. The two tactics which are used to subvert it, moreover, are to critique it intellectually (using post-structuralism), and to make it multi-ethnic. This helps to dilute the ideological and political aftertaste, but only just.

In high art *à la* Breker, though, the same tendencies are at work. For the neo-classicism of extreme Left and Right in the 20th century, as well as nearly all socially authoritarian tendencies worldwide, take a similar form. The West's contemporary way of dealing with this material is to reduce it to mere entertainment. The other way is to describe Breker as a great copyist—a slightly rigid and neo-conservative Rodin, for example.

This tendency tends to overlook the fact that Breker knew virtually everyone in the Arts—including Braque, Picasso, and all the others. There is a famous picture of Picasso's and Breker's dealers sitting together after the war, albeit with a print of Picasso's *Guernica* behind them. This is all part of a revisionist interpretation less of history than of art in the 20th century. No genuine artist or critic has ever disprivileged the Classical tradition or inheritance—Breker himself closely aligned with Dalí and Fuchs (of the neo-Realist Viennese school derived from Surrealism).

The truth of the matter is that artistic sensibility has always, sometimes in a secretive way, been involved with the far Right throughout the last century—at least metaphorically. What has happened is that creative people have had to survive or ride the tiger during a welter of destruction, that's all. This is why Wyndham Lewis could encompass *Hitler* (virtually banned everywhere now) and *The Hitler Cult* within a decade.

But enough of this . . . I wish to close by describing one particular painting by Frazetta. It is called *The Brain* and appears to be a watercolor. It was produced in the '60s and was used by the rock band Nazareth as a cover. To my mind, I think that Frazetta builds up the image slowly, foregrounds it, and then centers after several washes. I don't think that he paints in oils, but I've never been able to inspect an original. Anyway, this image shows a mastodonic, nay devilish warrior, in a horned Nordic helmet, and smiting a curved sword or scimitar, as it pounds down on another desperado who defends his body with a tensed shield.

Behind both of them, and proximate to a blood-red or purple ground, there pulsates an enormous brain: it's livid, secthing, multi-textured in its non-lobotomy, and pitted like the surface of the moon. It conjures up the image from a Marvel comic called *Tomb of Dracula*, drawn by Gene Colan, which features a villain known as Doctor Sun. He happens to be just a brain in a Plexiglas box.

But what does it all mean, I hear you cry? Why, the answer is quite clear: just ask a member of U.S. Navy SEALs, the British SAS, the French Foreign Legion, the Russian elite Special Forces, or, more controversially, the Waffen SS what it alludes to. It's an idealized statement of their inner life, that's all!

Counter-Currents/*North American New Right*
November 19, 2010

DOC SAVAGE
& CRIMINOLOGY

One of the more interesting things about the pulp star Doc Savage, the man of bronze, is that he carried out operations on the brains of criminals in order to correct them. These exercises in popular culture—the 181 pulp novels written by Lester Dent—are thus one of the most basic advocates for eugenics throughout the 1930s and '40s.

It is also interesting to note, *en passant*, that Doc Savage is referenced by an old Kansan in Truman Capote's famous non-fiction novel *In Cold Blood*, where it is suggested that the two desperadoes who murder the Clutter family could have their brains operated on to make them more docile and less violent, hence saving them from the scaffold. None of this came to pass (obviously). Yet the very fact that one could suggest—without shock and horror—that criminals could be experimented on in this way shows you the sharply divergent mores of the hour.

This is more than enough to set a keen observer thinking about the two distinct approaches to criminology which still reverberate today.

The first, which we could call the New Left approach, envisages crime as totally mediated by the social. Criminals are made and not born. The greater the amount of fiscal inequality in a society, the higher the preponderance of crime. This eventually locks itself into a *reductio ad absurdum* where, in a text like Foucault's *Discipline and Punish*, the more severe the penology the more vicious the crime you get as a result.

In this Leftist schema, crime is essentially deserved—it is a form of societal vengeance on the bourgeois class. Of course, in societies where the fissures are more racial than social, then the corresponding class biases in discussion of crime become racial ones instead. This brew makes the issue even more toxic to the liberal mind than hitherto.

The other great polarity in this debate is provided by what

we might call a New Right discourse — some of whose ideas are very ancient indeed — and streak back to the origins of criminology as a subject in 1876 when Cesare Lombroso published *Criminal Man*. This viewpoint sees crime as sociobiological in aspect. According to its register, criminals are born and not made, and although there may not be a criminal gene, as such, an absence of oxygen to the brain at birth in certain cases, together with the fact that widespread criminal families exist, tends to posit a physical basis to the criminaloid.

This ramifies with the recurrent idea of abnormality and lowness being a part of the criminal urge; whereby it can be seen that around a third of all mug shots in Black Museums or Encyclopedias of murder are grossly abnormal. Many criminals are habitual recidivists.

They repeat their offenses because they want to; they enjoy doing so; and criminality can be perceived as a lifestyle choice. Recurrent bouts of imprisonment then become a source of pride rather than the reverse.

In this outlook, a whole cluster of criminal attitudes go together, such as the belief that morality is about getting away with it, rape is normal sex, working is an idiot's game, lying is as natural as talking, and that the social order is only there to be exploited or taken advantage of.

If at the heart of the criminal subclass, criminals are born and not made, this revolutionizes criminology as a subject. It also opens up the way for experimentation on criminals who show the most pronounced symptoms of abnormality. By this viewpoint, criminality goes much deeper than amorality, heedlessness, the retention of an adolescent attitude into adult life, and so forth. It is no longer about alienation or rage. Nor is it a personal rebellion against society. Likewise, the criminal can never again be depicted as a victim of a harsh or unjust social order.

A large part of criminality is linked to anti-creativity and destructiveness as an end in itself. Erich Fromm's *The Anatomy of Human Destructiveness* is a key text here. The front cover of the 1980s paperback edition in Europe showed an Old Master painting which had been damaged by knife or razor slashes.

This related to a real series of mutilations and attacks on great paintings throughout Europe during that decade. Many of these attacks were copycat efforts, given the chronic uncreativity of the criminal mind. They also led to the institution of security models which you see in all galleries to this day.

The anatomy of human destructiveness views destruction and anti-creativity as a creativity. It wishes to destroy because it's there. This rubric is difficult for most people to grasp, since the wish to destroy, as a tainted death instinct, as an end in itself, is alien to most normally constituted people.

A moral heightening, however, can lead to a greater awareness of this negative trope, and certain criminals can undergo traumatic instants of moral remorse. This is the prospect of renewal about which all moralists preach. Could such a redemptive urge be prescribed to order — through the use of chemicals or brain operations, if and when the science has caught up with the speculation, and enables us to do so?

"Who knows?" is the honest answer to this. But, as always, fiction has already stolen a march on us. Let us imagine a scenario where not only Doc Savage in the 1930s but many heroes of a contemporary vintage advocate eugenics as a progressive end-point for crime. It would literally provide a bone-shaking jolt to contemporary mores.

After all, eugenics began as essentially a leftist orientation prior to the era in which Lester Dent (Kenneth Robeson) had Clark Savage, Junior and the Amazing Five — Monk, Ham, Johnny, Renny, and Long Tom — strut their stuff. If ever these attitudes return to popular culture then you will know that you are living through a seismic alteration in judgment.

Counter-Currents/*North American New Right*
September 13, 2011

CRIMINOLOGY, ELITISM, NIHILISM:
JAMES HADLEY CHASE'S
NO ORCHIDS FOR MISS BLANDISH

No Orchids for Miss Blandish was published in 1939 and later appeared in British editions by Robert Hale. Two films were made as a result of it (one of them by Robert Altman), and the Corgi/Transworld paperback editions have been sold all over the world. Millions upon millions of this book have been disseminated in pulp, cheap-papered editions in supermarkets and dime store racks. George Orwell was so shocked by it that he penned the famous essay "Raffles and Miss Blandish" as a consequence.

At this date, the provocative thing about this volume is its genuinely transgressive dimension in a world that exhibits multiple *frissons*. One of the most celebrated strategies in postmodernity is to "shock," irrespective of quality or content. In the mid-'70s a conceptual artist called Manzoni marketed his own ordure in a beautifully crafted, gilded box. It was wrapped in gold leaf and lapis lazuli (an Ezra Pound favorite). What could be more "anti-social" than this? An Italian-American heiress bought it for $7,000 so that she could boast about it at trendy parties. Nonetheless, Chase's pulp novel — which he put down on paper in under six weeks — is genuinely beyond the Pale of Dublin.

Most hard-boiled or realistic depictions of criminality end up romanticizing the criminal. They cannot help but do this, since if they're too brutal then commercial laws are defied. Also, the artistic or representational view of crime is slightly abstracted, Romantic, existential, and darkly macabre. *No Orchids* flouts all of these in several ways. There is an instinctual understanding of criminality or the lower depths here — quite independently of any socially conservative theories floated down the last century by Lombroso, Eysenck, Koestler, and most of the Behavioral School.

Chase sees lower criminality as ingrained, self-maturated, biological, and innate. There is no notion of social conditioning. Amongst these low and primitive specimens there may be a hierarchy, but it is strictly circumscribed to a subsidiary chasm: an underworld. This evaluation is most marked in Chase's treatment of the Grissom gang. All of them — from the ferocious matriarch Ma Grissom down to her psychopathic son Slim — are ethically dead.

What do we mean by this? Essentially all of them, the criminal women as well, view rape as normal sex, sadistic cruelty as a means to an end, and murder as rough horseplay engaged in for minute-to-minute gain, usually financial. Truly, for nearly all of the criminals in this book, hatred is love — it is the norm in all circumstances.

Quite contrary to the Left humanist view, crime is never considered to be socially conditioned. Inequality and the squalor of the slums have nothing to do with it. The Frankfurt School notion, repeated *ad nauseam* for over a century now, that criminality is a justified vengeance against a repressive bourgeois order, falls away. Here the naked and primordial order (or disorder) of a colony of killer apes comes into the foreground.

For James Hadley Chase and tough-minded or hard-boiled authors of his ilk see these things as biological *tout court*. It seems to denote the causation of Frank Norris' *McTeague* or Stroheim's *Greed* in its social Darwinian analysis, but without the literary or artistic pretensions. Indeed, this material has no desire to be considered as literature at all.

The other remarkable element to Chase's analysis is that — for his predatory troupe — everything is sexually motivated. This fits in very well with the polymorphously perverse testament *Psychopathia Sexualis* by Count Richard von Krafft-Ebing from the middle of the 19th century. Such an analysis imbues the biological, somatic, or genetic origins of primeval crime.

We are not talking about opportunistic criminality here, but the fate of those who were born to be criminal, itself a recognition that criminaloids are a Type. They are born and not made. Rather than an incidental sideline, adolescent fixation, and psychic fluidity, an almost constant erotomania is a semi-permanent feature. No concept of self-restraint even exists.

The core of the novel is the forcing of "dope" or drugs (probably mixtures of morphine and amphetamine) onto Blandish by Ma Grissom. This is so her psychopathic son, Slim, who is impotent and incapable of normal relations, can rape her repeatedly in a sub-pedophiliac way. (Note: one utilizes this term because she is reduced to a child-like dependency here. The Michael Jackson tendencies of Slim Grissom are admitted to by Chase at the novel's commencement.)

Blandish is the only wholly innocent character in the book. She is virtually a childlike *patina* onto which the other characters project their inadequacies.

Another salient point is the complete absence of any feminist input: There is no difference between criminaloid men or women in this regard. The two female arch-criminals, Ma Grissom and Anna Bork, behave exactly like their male colleagues in every respect. Moreover, Blandish's suicide at the end of the book is solely to get away from their influence, even after she's been released from the gang by the authorities.

In the course of the book's *dénouement* all of the criminals are exterminated by private detectives, uniformed police (Bulls in cant or criminal jargon), and G-men under Hoover. No mercy is shown; the human rights of the Grissom gang, for example, hardly exist in the consciousness of these law enforcers. Slim Grissom, dead inside and bored (even) with his catalog of molestations and murders, goes down in a hail of police fire. He expected no better. There is no redemption. Life is a fix. To him, every life is just an evacuation in Life's toilet bowl. Truly, as he falls to the dirt covered in blood, the result of FBI men bringing him down with machine-gun fire, he knew the meaningless of it all.

It is interesting to note that, despite all of the liberal humanist 'plaints to the contrary, three quarters of all criminals reoffend within a year of release from prison. Also, a half of all crime is committed again and again by the same hard core who exist in open-ended criminal families. They exist in all races, groups, and subsets . . . although about a third of all Western crime is committed by immigrants. Yet hardly any contemporary politicians ever mention the reality of criminality to their electorates, preferring to blather about rehabilitation instead.

Perhaps the provocative point to realize is that the masses share James Hadley Chase's view of crime—even as they sate on its presentation as entertainment.

Couldn't this be construed as an object lesson in pessimistic mass psychology being much more accurate than that of an Enlightenment elite which preaches "reform"? Finally, in ultra-Liberal England, where the death penalty was abolished 50 years back, 82% still support it. They entertain no illusions.

For those who have ears to hear—let them hear!

Counter-Currents/*North American New Right*
November 7, 2010

MECHANICAL FRUIT:
THE STRANGE CASE OF ANTHONY BURGESS' *A CLOCKWORK ORANGE*

A Clockwork Orange is a short novella produced by Anthony Burgess in a very short period of time—yet the author had doubtless dwelt upon an entire zoology before producing it. One of the book's characteristics, which even the most casual reader notices, is the experimental language or deliberate argot that Burgess develops for his retinue of juvenile delinquents. They speak, stutter, roll around in their own minds, and tend to use words like hammers, meat hooks, or early morning razor blades.

The story essentially revolves around the leadership principle or alpha dog mentality of Alex (the leader of this violent troupe of hoodlums) and its subjection to Skinnerian Behaviorism—a technique of which Burgess is highly critical. Paradoxically, Burgess is a highly moral and cross-grained man—a believing Catholic for most of his life—who worried extraordinarily about this novel's reception. For—to be sure—a short work which appeared to endorse or celebrate gang violence was the last thing that Burgess, a socially conservative Catholic, meant to bring to the table.

Another provocative trope—irrespective of the furor about Kubrick's later film and its withdrawal in Britain—was the Soviet influence on the entire production. Soviet, I hear you ask? Yes, that's right; for the germ from which the novel springs was a trip Burgess and his wife made to the Soviet Union in which they discovered a great deal of gang violence. This surprised both of them, but it shouldn't have really. Communist systems have a nuanced attitude towards criminality—for what they really fear, oppose, and act against are political crimes or the ideas that give rise to them.

This was by no means an original precept. In Alexander Solzhenitysn's *The Gulag Archipelago*, vol. 1, the world's most famous anti-Soviet dissident noticed an indulgence by the guards towards the *lags* or general prisoners, a latitude that would not be extended towards other *zeks*.

As in Orwell's *Nineteen Eighty-Four*, the Soviets treated the proles as near-animals, and their antics—youth cults, transgressive dress, drug usage, relative disrespect for Soviet authority—were all given remarkable indulgence. Why was this, Burgess wondered?

It probably had to do with two factors: first, the fact that crime was always less important than politics; and, secondly, that the party really fed upon itself, in that the lives of inner and outer party members—as in *Nineteen Eighty-Four*—were held to be far more important than those of mere proles. They were literally left to go to the dogs in every imaginable way—itself completely contrary to the official proletarian discourse of love and inclusion for the downtrodden, etc.

Another factor which Burgess cleverly makes use of is the introduction of communist words, phrases, and tags (gobbets of agitprop and so forth) in order to tease out and make more real the lingo of his various Youthies or violent adolescent pups.

Yet having said all of this, the real point of Burgess' short and linguistically-charged work was an attack on the way in which Alex and his *droogs* (pals) are reoriented or forced into well-adjusted behavior by the "system." Much of this, in turn, related to radical (if largely conservative commentators at the time) who wished to break the juvenile delinquency of the '50s by applying eugenic measures. (Note: Following Bowden, I would describe these behaviorist measures as dysgenic rather than the reverse, but there is no agreed definition here.)

What Burgess quite clearly objects to here is state-imposed morality. The way in which he dramatizes this is quite original—in that Alex, the Caesar of his gang, loves classical music, and the reconditioning causes him to loathe his former joy (Beethoven, etc.). Yet this is one of Burgess' own mistakes—given that the Droogs bear a striking similarity to the British subculture known as the Mods. Can you imagine a Quadraphonic (*sic*) subculturalist who prefers Colin Ireland to, say, *The Who*?

Yet Burgess definitely has a point here, in that the destructive side of behaviorist intervention was in its infancy then — although Burgess, with much greater insight than more "progressive" commentators, realizes that much of the gang's behavior is innate, biological, pre-social, or somatic in character.

But if the propensity to anti-social violence is innate, biological, pre-social, or somatic in character, this may lead us to conclude that some form of national service in Britain, France, Russia, etc. is vitally necessary for around at least 40% (and more) of the young male population. If you fold this proposition out a bit, then even Anthony Burgess would have to do it — along with all bourgeois and proletarian males who were not mentally impaired or physically ill. Heaven forbid!

Now many commentators might consider this to be just another form of invasive procedure — possibly less invasive but in no way less "demeaning" than the technique used in Burgess' *A Clockwork Orange*. This would certainly veer it into territory covered by Alan Sillitoe in the '50s (say) or a grainy, black-and-white film called *The Hill* (about British military prison or the glasshouse) and that starred young versions of Stanley Baker and Sean Connery. Nonetheless, these procedures are mass oriented, somatic, physical, and work on the external trappings of young males — almost in a semi-anthropological way. They lack the internal craft, guile — or cruelty — of Burgess' behaviorism and criminology in his short novel.

The point here is that they limit Alex's internal freedom of choice in relation to his passion for classical music. They are malefic in an intentional, *a priori*, or willed manner — partly due to the individualism of the punishment, the latter personally selected to match with the trainee's particularities.

Ultimately then, Burgess' fable revolves around the endless argument between free will and intentionality at the heart of Western thinking. (Note: even the Chorus in Aeschylus' *Agamemnon* debates whether Clytemnestra's murder of her husband is entirely self-elected or an inevitable outcome of Zeus' will.) It is always there. Burgess is a conservative and a pessimist — he is an Augustinian child. He believes that the punishment follows after the facts, is self-limiting and does not seek to change human nature. Man cannot change — he can just learn to endure better.

Arthur Kingsley Wake
"Anthony Burgess' *A Clockwork Orange*"
Counter-Currents/*North American New Right*
March 18, 2011

GEORGE ORWELL'S
NINETEEN EIGHTY-FOUR

George Orwell's *Nineteen Eighty-Four* is probably the most important political novel of the 20th century, but the Trotskyite influence on it is underappreciated. The entire thesis about the Party's totalitarianism is a subtle mixture of libertarian and Marxist contra Marxism ideas. One of the points which is rarely made is how the party machine doubles for fascism in Orwell's mind — a classic Trotskyist ploy whereby Stalinism is considered to be the recrudescence of the class enemy. This is of a piece with the view that the Soviet Union was a deformed workers' state or happened to be Bonapartist or Thermidorian in aspect.

Not only is Goldstein the dreaded object of hatred — witness the Two Minutes' Hate — but this Trotsky stand-in also wrote the evil book, *The Theory and Practice of Oligarchical Collectivism,* against which the party defines its existence. The inner logic or dialectic, however, means that the Inner Party actually wrote the book so that it would control the mainsprings of its own criticism.

One of the strongest features of *Nineteen Eighty-Four* is its use of what Anthony Burgess called "sense data." These are all the unmentionable things — usually realities in the physical world — which make a novel physically pungent or real to the reader. This is the very texture of life under "real existing socialism": scraping oneself in the morning with a bar of old soap, the absence of razor blades, human hair blocking a sink full of dirty water; the unsanitary details of conformism, socialist commerce, and queuing which made the novel feel so morally conservative to its first readers. This and the depiction of the working class (or proles), who are everywhere treated as socially degraded beasts of burden. Some of the most fruity illustrations come from Winston Smith's home flat in Victory Mansions — the smell of cabbage, the horrid nature of the Parsons' children, the threadbare and decrepit nature of everything, the continuous droning of the telescreen.

Most of these "sense data" are based on Britain in 1948. It is the reality of Wyndham Lewis' *Rotting Hill*—a country of ration cards, depleted resources, spivdom, dilapidated buildings after wartime bombing, rancid food, restrictions, blunt razor blades, and almost continuous talk about Victory over the Axis powers. Britain's post-war decline dates from this period when the national debt exceeded outcome by seven times—and this was before the joys of Third World immigration which were only just beginning. The fact that *Nineteen Eighty-Four* is just the conditions in Britain in 1948—at the level of the senses—is a fact not widely commented on.

The uncanny parallels between Newspeak and political correctness are widely mentioned but not really analyzed—save possibly in Anthony Burgess' skit *1985*, a satire which majors quite strongly on proletarian or workers' English—whereby every conceivable mistake, solecism, mispronunciation, or scatology is marked up; correct usage is everywhere frowned upon.

Another aspect of the novel which receives scant attention is its sexological implications. In most coverage of *Nineteen Eighty-Four*, the party organization known as the Anti-Sex League is given scant attention. Yet Orwell had considerable theoretical overlaps with both Fromm and Wilhelm Reich—never mind Herbert Marcuse. Orwell's thesis is that totalitarianism fosters a sexless hysteria in order to cement its power. The inescapable corollary is that more liberal systems promote pornography and promiscuity in order to enervate their populations.

Orwell certainly pinpointed the arrant puritanism of Stalinist censorship—something which became even more blatant after the Second World War. One also has to factor in the fact that Orwell was living and writing in an era where importing James Joyce's *Ulysses* and Henry Miller's *Tropic of Cancer* were criminal offenses. Nonetheless, Orwell's anti-puritanism and libertarianism, sexually speaking, is very rarely commented on. Perhaps this leads to the nakedly sexual rebellion of Winston and Julia's affair against the Party. A series of actions for which the mock Eucharist, the imbibing of bread and wine in O'Brien's inner party office, will not give them absolution!

It might also prove instructive to examine the sequences of

torment which Winston Smith has to undergo in the novel's last third. This phase of the book is quite clearly Hell in a Dantesque triad (the introductory section in Victory Mansions and at the Ministry is Purgatory, and Heaven is the brief physical affair with Julia). In actual fact, well over a third of the novel is expended in Hell, primarily located in the fluorescent-lit cells of the Ministry of Love.

This is the period where O'Brien comes into his own as the party inquisitor or tormentor, an authorial voice in The Book, and a man who quite clearly believes in the system known as Ingsoc, English Socialism. He is a fanatic or true believer who readily concedes to the Party's inner nihilism and restlessness: "If you want a picture of the future, imagine a boot stamping on a human face—for ever."

Moreover, the extended torture scene and was quite clearly too much for many readers—in north Wales, one viewer of the BBC drama in the mid-'50s dropped dead during the rat scene. I suppose one could call it the ultimate review! Questions were even asked in parliament about what a state broadcaster was spending its money on.

Nonetheless, O'Brien is quite clearly configured as a party priest who is there to enforce obedience to the secular theology of Ingsoc. (Incidentally, Richard Burton is superb as O'Brien in the cinematic version of the novel made in the year itself, 1984.)

The point of the society is to leave the proles to their own devices and concentrate entirely on the theoretical orthodoxy of both the inner and outer party members. In this respect, it resembles very much a continuation of the underground and Bohemia when in power. You get a whiff of this at the novel's finale, with Winston ensconced in the Chestnut Tree Café waiting for the bullet and convinced of his love for Big Brother.

This is the inscrutable face of the Stalin lookalike which stares meaningfully from a hundred thousand posters in every available public place. Might he be smiling under the mustache?

Counter-Currents/*North American New Right*
July 1, 2011

EUGENICS OR DYSGENICS?
BRIAN ALDISS' *MOREAU'S OTHER ISLAND*

Moreau's Other Island by the science fiction writer Brian Aldiss was published over 30 years ago, but it still retains a certain "bite" in sociobiological terms.

It obviously rewrites H. G. Wells' *The Island of Dr. Moreau* from the 1880s, which, in and of itself, was one of the most magisterial examinations of all the moral questions around vivisection that had ever been penned (certainly up to that date). Aldiss definitely outdoes the moralizing of John Cowper Powys' novelistic treatment, *Morwyn: Or the Vengeance of God*, and the only books with which it can be usefully compared are non-fictional. These were Savitri Devi's *Impeachment of Man* and Professor Peter Singer's *Animal Liberation*.

Brian Aldiss' work examines a senior American government official or bureaucrat, Calvert Roberts, who has no idea that the island he plummets down onto is actually conducting experiments sponsored by his very own State Department. It is a classic example of the German sociologist Max Weber's Iron Cage: where the left hand in administration chooses not to know what the right hand is doing, deliberately so . . . These vivisections go way beyond the original Doctor Moreau (renamed McMoreau in this narrative—and perceived of as a real character rather like T. H. Huxley, Wells' old mentor). The purpose was, first, to replicate human-animal hybrids; then to experiment with limblessness and the extreme plasticity of the human shape; and finally to develop a new species, humanoids, who would be resistant to fallout and radiation after a nuclear war. Such a cataclysm is just beginning in the novel's earliest pages.

The interesting thing to note is that variants on all of these experiments have been done. The latter two stages as computer simulations (to my knowledge); and the primary area has definitely been realized. Scientists all over the world, but primarily in the West, have created both human-animal hybrids and mortal-plant-admixtures. It is also interesting to note that dysgenic or anti-ethical experimentation, biologically speaking, has been conducted by virtually every political regime on earth — especially the Federal government in the United States.

Note: for these purposes I am using "eugenics" in the way Galton originally proposed, meaning positive and legal interventions that break no generic law at the present time and that intend to reduce disease, boost life chances, and improve or maximize Mankind's nature, somatically. Most bioethicists approve of these procedures with one or two quibbles, although pro-life and religiously motivated ethicists object to many procedures in biological science *per se*.

Dysgenics — for the purpose of this review — means transgressive or illegal procedures that go beyond what is permitted, often fueled by a particular interpretation of Nietzscheanism, and that many scientists are addicted to. They call it pushing the envelope or boundaries, and, in fictional guise, Wells had Moreau describe it as "the pure colorless joy of unlimited research." It has to be said that most biological scientists have this viewpoint, although few of them have the courage to articulate it in the wider society.

Metapolitical sensitivities are still relatively raw here — although eugenics is usually associated with some of the biological management program in Europeanist and revolutionary Germany between 1933 and 1945. Much of this material, in turn, has been sublimated and exteriorized in *The Boys from Brazil* sort of way. Nonetheless, the Clinton administration paid out $90 million in reparations to poor White Americans and Black ex-cotton pickers in both Utah and the Deep South. It appears that nuclear radiation was deliberately leaked to test its effects on civilians in the Mormon state; and that various Negroes were irradiated, and injected with syphilis and other diseases, in order to test their effects. Indeed, dysgenic research — primarily sponsored by the CIA and what the Left-wing dissident Noam Chomsky would call the military-industrial complex (*sic*) — only formally ended under the Nixon administration in 1972. This was most evident in the program known as MK-ULTRA which carried out destabilizing, devitalizing, fringe, extremist, and "edge of darkness" behavioral experiments throughout the era of the high Cold War.

As Freudianism faded amongst hard scientists in psychology—witness H. J. Eysenck's *Decline and Fall of the Freudian Empire*—various security bureaucracies became obsessed with Skinnerian behaviorism. This was the sort of Maoism-in-reverse formula where humans could be completely reprogrammed to do violent acts, assassination for example, as a result of brainwashing, reconditioning, and reflexiveness to prior stimuli.

Many of these notions fueled the anti-psychiatric movement at the latter end of the 20th century—epitomized by R. D. Laing, for instance. Most of these techniques are now known to be completely flawed—Man is too complicated to be reducible to such simplistic programming, rewiring and formulaic/stock responses. Yet the British state itself was heavily involved in Skinnerian "torture" experiments against Axis spies in North Africa during the Second World War (1939-1945).

Today, most Western countries deliberately contract out such "dubious" or "black" activities to Third World partners where there is little media intrusion. Also, as part of the recent Al-Qaeda emergency or "War on Terror," the U.S. has established "black" sites all over the world: in Algeria, Tunisia, Poland, the Czech Republic, etc. . . .

Actually, I mention this not to demonize any particular regime. My metaphysically conservative and ontologically pessimistic view is that virtually every form of state (including liberal-humanist regimes) carry on in this way.

Incidentally, the British behavioral-cum-dysgenic experiments were conducted in Egypt, near Cairo, at SIME (Secret Intelligence Middle East) by Doctor Alexander Kennedy on behalf of SIS/MI6. The subjects were always non-European (much like French special forces in their war against the Algerian FLN later on) in what the great historian Alistair Horne called *A Savage War of Peace: Algeria, 1954-1962*.

It is also important to point out that such experiments are kept secret even within bureaucracies—this is partly designed to give politicians plausible deniability. Also, many senior figures in security bureaucracies fiercely oppose such measures.

Dick White, an upper-class Englishman of the old school and a deputy director of MI6 in the 1940s, wrote a scathing report about Kennedy's experiments which he regarded as amateurish and counterproductive. He considered them to be the work of quacks and sadists.

Similarly, virtually 100% of the British interrogators at SIME who dealt with German and Italian prisoners (quite fairly as it turned out) knew nothing of these experiments. Spies — unlike Axis combatants from a legal point of view — remain uncovered by most laws of war and the Geneva Convention. All that prevents the most grotesque abuses is the fear of what rival intelligence bureaucracies might do to one's own agents (as it were).

But to return to Aldiss' fiction: one of the most original features in this narrative is the characterization of the Moreau figure, Mortimer Dart, who makes his appearance in the chapter, "In the Hands of the Master." Unusually for science fiction, the inner or psychological motivation for his vivisections is well sketched. For Aldiss presents Dart as a thalidomide victim.

Thalidomide was a drug that the *Sunday Times* went outside the law in order to expose in the early 1960s. It was designed to ease morning sickness in pregnant women, but actually led to gross abnormalities in the unborn child. These — almost after the fashion of a medical thriller writer like Robin Cook — involved the stunting of the arms and legs . . . although it has been widely noted that many thalidomide victims have led happy and successful lives. Quite a few commentators have remarked on this. Could it be because they were mentally predisposed to be able-bodied — to make use of "politically correct" jargon over disability?

Nonetheless, Aldiss portrays Dart as filled with a misanthropic rage due to his affliction, and, it has to be said, that your average James Bond villain pales in comparison to the relative sophistication the author shows here. Mortimer Dart also wears a prosthetic suit — much like Doctor Octopus in *Spiderman* — from which he reaches out in order to grapple with and master the world.

Over time Calvert becomes more and more rebellious, loses the spark of his early Christianity, and even sides with the

Beast people against Dart. Despite their bestiality and relative danger to him, these half-animals are better — in this American administrator's eyes — than the post-humanoids whom the U.S. government wants Professor Dart to create. Aldiss clearly shares this view — but only just.

He is too much of a scientist *manqué* — if we consider science fiction to be an imaginative conduit for many rationalists — to completely give up on this dysgenesis. Like a painter with a blank canvas before him, the pure or research scientist always thinks that the next experiment will be the one that leads to the greatest illumination. Nothing else matters: to paraphrase the original Moreau, way back in the 19th century, "I ceased to having a bleeding mass of pain before me (a vivisected animal) and conceived of it only as a problem. And once I had liberated it from its form . . . why, what did I have? Another problem . . ." Wells, who began as a biological experimenter, knew exactly what he was talking about here. Prendick, the protagonist in Wells' tale, objects to Doctor Moreau's effusions — but the great scientist merely raises his hand to silence him.

The question, "Do you think that Science has anything to do with Humanism?" seems to be implicit in Moreau's gesture. There have actually been so many variants of these debates in the real world — and the physical realities that they have led to — that it is difficult to know where to begin. One example of such a parallelism (most definitely) is Israel's attempts to create genetic or ethnic weapons — the so-called racial bomb. These would be microbial agents designed to attack and kill only Arabs. The problem for the Zionist state has been twofold; weaponization; and the fact that at least 40% of the citizenry inside the Israeli republic could be targeted by such a device.

At the close of Aldiss' fable there is a condition of stasis or unresolved tension. Both Dart and Calvert (irrespective of their different moral responses) are rescued from the island by distinct parts of the American federal government. The Navy (and hence the Pentagon) rescues Dart, the limbless experimenter on the margins of flesh, and Calvert is airlifted from this fumarole by dint of a State Department helicopter. Aldiss is a fictionalist — an artistic writer; not a philosopher. One also presumes (doubtlessly) that at another level he just wanted to rewrite one of the most famous books ever written in his genre. Yet a sort of theoretical residue is left once the plot's violent catharsis is over — a writer like Ray Bradbury, to my mind, often achieves this as well.

Possibly Aldiss is hinting in *Moreau's Other Island* that the onrushing speed of biological developments will crush most ideological and ethical speculations in their path. Certainly, most notions of socialism, communism, radical or Left-liberalism, an equality agenda enforced by PC norms, Left or egalitarian anarchism, Christian ethics, Humanism, liberalism or feminism are rejected out of hand by Biologism.

Biology now dwarfs the other physical sciences and increasingly bestrides the other disciplines like a colossus. Each and every issue when put to a purely somatic test — comes down with Konrad Lorenz in *On Aggression* and against Kropotkin's views about mutual aid. For, even if altruism is hard-wired, this itself confirms the supremacy of living matter and its norms.

One faces the inescapable conclusion that every tendency in Western society runs counter to biological fanaticism — with the sole possibility of market-worship, the cult of beauty (even in commercial pornography), and the adoration of success.

Yet maybe this is the New Left's last hurrah? According to Brian Aldiss' dystopian fiction there are only two options — eugenics or dysgenics. This completely revolutionizes the left-right split, in accordance with Nietzsche's gnomic diction in the posthumous notebooks, *The Will to Power*, when he declared that life is a matter of breeding.

It is also interesting to note that many extreme Right-wingers now, if the only option were eugenics or dysgenics, would actually choose the former — thence putting themselves on the liberal side of a merciless biologism, i.e., with Calvert against Dart. This isn't at all unintentionally ironic, since the eugenics movement in the early part of the 20th century was nearly all Leftist (completely counter-intuitively to received wisdom today).

In Western Europe especially, where mass religion has virtually died out, with the sole exception of immigrant communities, and scientific materialism measures its own wasteland: what's your choice? Eugenics or dysgenics?

What! Cat got your tongue? Perhaps, *passim*. Aldiss' other novel in a similar vein, *Frankenstein Unbound*, there is no cat—only a tongue!

Counter-Currents/*North American New Right*
January 17, 2011

Francis Pollini's *Night*

Francis Pollini's *Night* was published by Olympia Press around 50 years ago and deals with the Korean War, but for all that it is still relevant. It concerns the Communist brainwashing techniques used by the Maoist Chinese forces on American prisoners of war during that conflict. These were based on various behaviorist ideas which were very much in the air at that time and were used extensively by the KGB, CIA, MI6, the French secret services, and other parallel or adjacent bodies.

The novel deals with a triumvirate of main characters over a 200-page span. The first is the Italian-American G.I. Marty Landi, the one serviceman who does not break as a result of the Chinese questioning; Phillips, the leader of the Resistance in the prison camp; and Ching, the diabolical Chinese interrogator.

These Maoist techniques were based on certain Chinese conceptions about the plasticity of consciousness. Man's mentality — particularly that of a prisoner of war — was considered to be extremely malleable and susceptible to toxic influences. The first thing to do was to remove all available authority figures. First, all of the accredited officers were taken away and put in other camps. Second, this went double for the non-commissioned officers who were technically closer to the men as raw recruits.

Once these nodal points for leadership had been silenced, the natural leaders were disposed of. These were individuals from amongst the general miscellany of men who evinced any capacity for independent judgment, creative tension or flair, ability to hold an audience, etc. They were then sent to the "Reactionaries" camp or compound.

What was left was an undifferentiated *mass* that could be attacked with behaviorist techniques. A considerable number of G.I.s — as admitted to by the Americans after the war — learned

Communist slogans in a lemming-like way and became inveterate enemies of Uncle Sam. A countercultural ideology of anti-American blame and defamation was built up by the Chinese to replace the pre-existing bonds of society and community.

It must have been something to see quite large numbers of Americans in these camps denouncing President Truman, America the war-monger, and the CAPITALIST BIG PIGS (*sic*), while unleashing paeans of praise toward Communist China and North Korea. After the war—on the release of these individuals—they were uneasily rehabilitated back into the United States, where an understandable desire to bury bad news prevented these stories from emerging.

These behaviorist techniques—mass persuasion, better rations and conditions, mutual group pressure, isolation from different or contesting viewpoints—all have a register on the individual level as well. These were brainwashing techniques used by all sides in the middle of the 20th century. Such torture trials were often carried out against spies, lone individuals, or people who had betrayed their own side.

One example is that afforded by Doctor Alexander Kennedy at SIME in the early 1940s in North Africa. SIME was Secret Intelligence Middle East (based in Cairo) and an essential hub for MI6 activity throughout the war. Several Axis spies—mostly Arabs—were subjected to behavioral conditioning and other forms of desensitization.

This involved isolation, being masked and forced to wear goggles as well as gloves of a special type, white noise experimentation, effective refusal to visit the bathroom, sleep deprivation, and high anxiety states induced by the use of amphetamines like Thyroxin. These were injected directly into the brain.

The purpose, according to a clinical sadist like Kennedy, was to achieve "a total breakdown in personality." The individual concerned would then be handed over to "normal" examiners or interviewers to provide them with whatever information they required.

Now these Maoist experiments in the early 1950s were on a much cruder and wider scale, but detailed relationships grew up between the G.I. submitted to torment (Landi) and the interrogator (Ching). Umberto Eco in his medieval novel *The Name of the Rose* talks about an insidious bond that develops between the inquisitor and his victim, and the same thing occurs here.

Initially, Landi manfully resists the Maoist techniques of entrapment with considerable courage and tenacity. He is determined to prove himself a Reactionary rather than a Progressive, but over time a kinship grows up between himself and Ching (unnatural as this may appear at first sight).

Ching attempts to exploit a personal debility in Landi, possibly a deep if buried reservoir of depression, and use it for his own purposes. What he basically wants to obtain is information about who has subtly organized the Reactionaries in their camp. This spills over into attacks on the pro-captor Progressives by those forces which Phillips, a reserve officer, has marshalled in America's defense.

There is no actual collusion. Landi never gives into Ching. Certainly there is no textual basis for this in the book, but the imputation is that the insidiousness of the brainwashing gets to Landi in the end. This, on release and return to the United States at the end of the book, leads to his presumed suicide.

Phillips, on the other hand, enacts a terrible vengeance on the Progressives by stealing down from his camp, amid the extreme cold of an Asian winter, and murdering seven of them with his bare hands. This includes Slater, the ringleader of the pro-Chinese and North Korean Americans among the Progressive faction. He—not atypically—happens to be Ching's favorite amongst the prisoners, with the sole exception of Marty Landi.

Landi, and a few of the others, seek shelter with the Chinese against the bitterness of the weather in the Reactionaries' compound. Yet Ching must be led to Phillips by a *reductio ad absurdum* at the end, given that he is left alone in the Reactionaries camp suffering from an acute fever after his forays in the icy cold. Phillips is later beheaded, and his severed head delivered to the surviving men of the Reactionary compound in a box.

The interesting thing about the novel is that it offers no hope, no way out, and no effective refutation of the Communist strategies. It is also written in a heavily demotic style, involving stream of consciousness and a lot of swearing, although, given the context, hardly any of this is gratuitous. I also don't think that there's been a mainstream edition since the New English Library one in the early 1970s. In any event, this novel is a poignant if grim epitaph to a pretty deplorable American episode.

Counter-Currents/*North American New Right*
August 12, 2011

Sarban's
The Sound of His Horn

Sarban was the Persian pseudonym of John William Wall (1910–1989), a relatively obscure British diplomat in the Middle East, who wrote five volumes of Gothic stories, short novels, plays, and the like. These were gathered together in the books *Ringstones* (1951), *The Sound of His Horn* (1952), *The Doll Maker* (1953), *The Sacrifice* (2002), and *Discovery of Heretics* (2010). Wall wrote relatively little and was a perfectionist who never expected publication. Our main point of departure will be *The Sound of His Horn*.

In his book-length essay, *New Maps of Hell*, Kingsley Amis examines the novel as a reactionary fantasy. Amis was quite well-known at this period for contrasting science fiction (of which he was a literary historian) against fantasy fiction. He believed the former to be progressive, optimistic, and utopian with a Center-Left bias; whereas fantasy was crabby, archaic, often rural in setting, reactive, and pessimistic. It habitually wore a conservative mask—irrespective of the intentions of the author. George Orwell's *Nineteen Eighty-Four* would be the classic example here—whereby a democratic socialist and former demi-Trotskyite wrote the most devastating anti-socialist dystopia ever conceived.

The Sound of His Horn is an anti-Nazi fable which is quite clearly complicitous with its subject—and this becomes more and more obvious as the narrative proceeds. In passing, it bears some relation to the critical *fabula*, *On the Marble Cliffs* by Ernst Jünger, a Right-wing critique of National Socialism, which is very much a fictionalization of the Conservative Revolution.

Superficially speaking, *The Sound of His Horn* is critical of fox-hunting and hunting in general, but this only occurs within the perspective of rural piety and a hunting fraternity of a highly conservative bent. In this novella the Germans are the winners of the Second World War which they have rechristened The War of German Rights. One presumes that this Sarban's allusion to the Confederate idea that the American Civil War was fought to secure States' Rights. This, in turn, opens up a link to some of those apologies for the Second German Empire which were penned by men like Houston Stewart Chamberlain at the height of the First World War (1914-18).

In Wall's novel, a ruling German caste has introduced fox-hunting with human beings as part of a post-war master-slave nexus. Although a rather callow conceit, Wall shows some genius in explicating his chosen theme, to which he endlessly returns. One thing which this novel displays all too obviously is that without either the occult or the far Right, these genres would be sadly impoverished — in terms of their own ability to harness fantasy or create it out of nothing at all. The novel certainly divides women into hunted birds and predatory cats — the latter part of a hunting fraternity led by a Göring lookalike. The thesis is one of Germanic/bucolic brutality — less the return of the repressed than of a Teutonic mastery given a new lease of life by technical outreach.

Yet it is quite clear that Sarban may be morally critical of this — as is made clear by the terrified breakdown of Alan Querdilion, the main character. But the author is quite clearly equivocal about the whole hunting enterprise due to the surprising levels of intimacy which grow up between pursuer and pursued, hunter and hunted, huntress and huntsman, victor and violator. According to the criminology of the Frankfurt School, human beings either identify with the victim or the oppressor — yet it is quite clear that Sarban does both, given his sadomasochistic sexuality.

There is such a desire to be polite about this in the literary criticism that one almost hesitates to bring it up — even though Kingsley Amis spends half his introduction to the Ballantine Books edition mulling it over. For it is quite clear that Sarban's literary interests become most engaged when this literary theme surfaces. In a sexological sense, Wall is divided and on both sides at once, as Querdilion experiences a banquet at the lodge, rural hunting by night, the use of humans as baboons and mock-birds, as well as the thrill of the chase at the end. Just prior to the electrified fence—a source of Boehlen rays—the Reich's master forester spares Querdilion in an act of feudal generosity and mercy born of satiation.

Yet what this novella really exemplifies is a fascination with the dark side, with everything "politically incorrect" long before this terminology entered common usage. Without the thrill of transgression or "inhumanism," much of liberal fiction and art would be completely flaccid and without any depth of characterization. It is the presence of the right/wrong side which makes it all worthwhile in the long-term. For, as Wall/Sarban gets more and more excited, amid a world of female birds and predatory cats, rampaging boar-hounds, and human prey, under the floodlights and next to the barbed wire—as the forces of the Reichs forester gets closer . . . one realizes a salient truth. And this is the fact that in a liberal order, the Right appears to be everywhere powerless—except in one's dreams. For the societies created out of Enlightenment nostrums have surrendered their entire unconscious *to the other side*.

Counter-Currents/*North American New Right*
December 1, 2010

The Real Meaning of Punch & Judy*

I'd like to talk about the English/Anglo-Italian tradition of Punch and Judy. Now, I saw Punch and Judy first when I was about four years old and almost everyone in Britain has seen it at some time or other. The first thing that strikes you about it is its color and its vigor and its moral/amoral violence. If you remember, it used to be down at the seaside pretty much, but it's now gone indoors as a sort of under-fives form of entertainment.

Now, the man that does Punch and Judy is called a Professor, and in working class or popular diction it's widely known that anyone who's bright about a particular issue, or could be said to be informed about it, is called a professor. So, anyone who talks with some degree of loquacity about anything, "Eh, you're a professor, mate!" and that sort of thing. That comes from Punch and Judy, the idea that the man who is in charge is the Professor.

The Professor is handed this role by a father figure or somebody before him, so it's an ancestral folk tradition. Traditionally in this craft art, you have to carve the puppets yourself, so that some of you enters into them as a thing, as a form.

If you notice, in the tall booths, which have got this sort of red and yellow awning on front, back, and sides, the Professor sits inside. So, the Professor is in quite a tall booth, which he has opened in the back so he can breathe easily on the seashore. There are two hands that go up above the level that a youngish or child-like audience is looking up towards.

You've got the two figures. Now, there's a sort of occultistic or mystical element to Punch and Judy because Punch is always on the right of the Professor (the left as people see it), but he's always on the right side of the Professor because Punch can never be killed. Punch can never be destroyed. Punch is always eternal.

---

*Transcription by V. S. of a lecture delivered at the 24th meeting of the New Right, London, November 21, 2009.

Punch is a grotesque. He has an enormous nose and has an enormous belly because he's been overeating, and he has an enormous hunchback. So, already there's an element of a sort of "medieval" cruelty to it. People laugh because he's deformed. As soon as he gets up on the stage people go, "ahahaha!" and they're laughing at him as well as with him.

His nemesis is Judy, of course, who comes up on the other side. Judy is a nag and comes from the *commedia dell'arte*. She also has an enormous nose, and sometimes an enormous belly as well. Sometimes their noses sort of lock horns like two beasts, and they move about the front of the stage. At other times, she's more sedentary. The position of the left-handed puppet is changeable because the left mutates and changes; politically, metapolitically, spiritually, it morphs.

And the whole point of much of the "killing" in Punch and Judy is that there has to be a mechanism to change the puppet on the left side all the time. So, Punch beats them to death! They come up, and they're beaten to death, and they go down again very quickly. There's a whole range of these puppets that come up, of which Judy is the first.

Now, all of these puppets are gloves with the exception of the baby, because Punch and Judy are a couple, even though they're really old and decrepit, and they've had a baby. The baby's on a stick with a small head. It's the only one that exists independently of the gloves. Traditionally, the baby is thrown into the audience in a particular scenario.

The audience is 5 to 15 to 25 to 90. In the 19th century and early 20th century, there would be enormous audiences. The children would be at the front and the adults, engaging in a slightly guilty pleasure, would be at the back.

Now, where did this tradition come from? The truth is it's almost eternal. Because these popular or folk forms that Richard Wagner and other major artists loved and built much of the elements of their art out of are immemorial. There are pictures from Anatolia, drawings a thousand years old, and they depict figures in a booth which look suspiciously like a chap with a large nose and a funny hat beating a nag. So, we sort of know that this tradition has existed in various ways and is reinvented.

Those who are aware of puppets will know there are two forms. There's the glove, and there's the marionette that moves from above with the strings. Everyone has seen Gerry Anderson's *Captain Scarlet* and *Thunderbirds* and *Joe 90* and all of these sort of heroic things when they were very young pretty much, and here we have a marionette that moves from above. That's very much the French tradition.

There's a man called the Bottler who has a top hat and a large trumpet, and he announces the festival. He announces *The Tragicomedy of Punch and Judy*, although it's usually just *The Play of Mr. Punch*, and all the children drag the parents, and all the parents are going "oh, God . . . ," but the children want to see it, so they drag them to the audience. The Bottler is so called because he controls the crowd, because it's a popular entertainment. It can be quite rough. If people don't like it they chuck stuff at the stage. Stray dogs come around and have to be chased off if you're outside.

Punch and Judy traditionally involves a dog called Toby. Remember Toby dog? Toby! And Toby's there, and he's on the top of the panel. He's very tame and so on, but he can become a bit less domesticated when another mutt turns up, because he knows he's got to defend the pitch. That's one of his roles, you see.

Now, this particular tradition that exists now — which has dipped down at various times and is having a bit of a revival, paradoxically, in the last 25 years when major concepts of Englishness have been under such deconstructive challenge — this tradition comes largely from the 1780s. An Italian showman who was believed to be illiterate settled in the East End of London and brought an attenuated version of the Italian playlet called *commedia dell'arte* over the channel and settled here. His name was Puccini, but he was known as Porcini by all of his followers. "Mr. Porcini and his travelling circus of freaks and shows!" He developed the modern tradition.

A man called J. P. Collier wrote a book about his type of theater in about 1818, and a very famous English artist called Cruikshank did engravings of all of the characters. Now, Cruikshank was a very major figure, equal to Hogarth and Rowlandson, and he's one of the most violent and famous cartoonists and caricaturists in English traditional art. The line, and the concepts of graphic energy in the line, is cardinal to a particular type of Anglo-Saxon creativity. One of the reasons that Puccini, amongst probably other showmen actually, is designated as the originator of the modern tradition, which is almost 250 years old now, is because an artist and a writer, Collier and Cruikshank, put it down.

Now, Punch is on the right here and can never be destroyed. Judy comes up. The baby also exists. There's a whole range of other characters. The discourse is modulated as to how adult the audience is and how much they can take.

One of the reasons that Judy and Punch nag each other is because he has a mistress. The mistress is called Pretty Polly, hence the term. Pretty Polly appears occasionally. Polly never speaks. She just sighs. She goes, "*Aaah, oooh, aaah,*" and she moves about. Punch moves around, circling like a shark, with his nose down and the hat waving, and this sort of thing.

But Judy is always about to appear, like in the French farce. She's always about to appear. The nose appears on the side of the stage and all the children go, "Ah, there she is!" She's back again when Polly's disappeared, you see. What the Professor is doing is every time a new character emerges he takes the glove down, he puts the glove on a hook which is underneath the rim of the stage that the audience can see, and brings up another character.

One of the other characters is Clown Joey, and Clown Joey is a zany, or a *zani* in the Italian version of the tradition, a Johnny. Joey is Punch's benevolent side. He can never be killed. He never speaks, but he's very irritating. He goes, "*mmm hmm mmm,*" and Punch says, "*Why are you doing that!? What are you doing that for!? It's very, very irritating!*" and, consequently, he wants to beat Joey to death. He intends to get Joey in various ways. Joey gets down. Joey runs to one side. "*I'm going to get you! I'm going to get you!*" And they go back and forth across the top of the stage. He can never kill Joey because Joey is his benevolent side. Now, Punch is sort of non-dualist and amoral and attacks everything and everybody. He's partly deaf, because he's old, and can't hear what people are saying.

Another character is Scaramouche. Now, Scaramouche comes up and is a differentiated version of Joey. He has a very long neck which he can extend out, out into the audience even. It's a trick of the puppet. You press a button inside it, and it comes out. Or it's just a pole that you sort of lever out from the side and people think in the speed of it that it's coming from the puppet. And all the children go, "Oh, look, look, look!" Of course, what Punch wants to do is break that neck or strangle him. So, he tries to get over him and strangle him, of course, but he's indestructible like Joey, his principle.

Another famous character is the Crocodile. The Crocodile appears, and he's green and has a very long snout with teeth. The Crocodile is a relative of the Dragon which existed in the mystery plays of the Middle Ages. The mystery plays typically involve a Christian icon, such as Saint George, beating the Dragon to death. The medieval idea being that the evil in the puppet is beaten out of the character. Now, often the Crocodile can morph into a Dragon, an older variant from the Middle Ages which has largely been discarded from the contemporary troupe, or he can become the Devil.

The Devil appears in Punch and Judy in red with horns. Whenever the Devil appears, the Bottler, whose the sort of middleman between the audience and the stage, goes, "*Oooooh, look! The Devil is here!*" and the Devil comes up. Initially, Punch is frightened of the Devil and runs about. Because you can have sort of distended perspective, if you like. Say I'm the Professor. You've got Punch here. You've got the stage there. The Devil emerges behind, and he's sort of on your shoulder, really. But you're down here so your head can't be seen. You move Punch across, and the Devil comes up, and everybody goes, "Oooooh!"

Traditionally, Dr. Johnson said in Boswell's biography of him, that Punch is always beating the Devil to death, but he's always beating everyone to death! Including the Minister! The Minister, or Priest, or Methodist as he's sometimes called, is the Christian figure who appears. His hands are glued together because he's so pious he's always praying, you see. He comes up, and he says, "*Dearly beloved, we all love Punch. Punch is a sinner. We pray*

The Real Meaning of Punch & Judy

for his reclamation." And Punch says, *"Shut up, you old fraud!"* and beats him over the back of head, and he goes back down under the top of the stage.

I first became very aware of the potency of this sort of tradition for people who are beyond five years of age when I attended an event of the British National Party which is called the Red, White, and Blue. Interestingly, they had a traditional Punchman from Lancashire, and the police came on the site to stop it. Very interesting! The police came on the site to stop it. And the reason that they said they were going to stop it is it didn't have an entertainment license.

This is how things are done in modern Britain. There is a sort of ideological overlay to this that these are just blokes obeying orders, and they say to you, "Look, don't be boring. We've got this thing to enforce. Obey it. We don't agree or disagree with it. We're merely functionaries. Just a pair of hands." That's the view that they have of themselves, essentially.

But in a way, if you look across England now, and Britain as an extension, an enormous number of our traditions (pubs, the circus, this sort of thing) are being disprivileged. It's being put down. It's as if it's not really wanted anymore. It's too *Ur* or too organic or too ethnically charged. There's a dangerous absence of minorities in the audience. It's slightly *exclusionist* by virtue of its program, even though it hasn't really sought that. It hasn't set out with the idea of being incorrect or exclusionist. It just is, because it relates to a prior period of identity.

This brings me on to the very politically incorrect elements of Punch and Judy beyond the "sexism" and the generalized beatings and the disableism and the animalism/speciesism and all of the things which I've just glossed.

One element is the racial element. All foreigners are funny. So, whenever a foreigner appears people howl with laughter. The Turk appears saying *"shalabah,"* and everyone howls with laughter. The Black Man, as we'll call him, appears and everyone howls with laughter. Immediately, Punch wants to kill him, as soon as he's appeared and leaps around and this sort of thing.

This tradition is called Jim Crow, which relates to a 19th century music hall tradition made very famous by Jim Thompson, an Edinburgh *artiste* and sort of music hall performer in around 1830. The whole tradition that morphs into human acting traditions and that gives rise to the Black and White minstrels, which were very current on mass popular television of the time when I was a child in the 1970s, this all dips down because it becomes self-consciously "offensive." In a sense, when it becomes self-conscious, due to the presence of the Other in its midst, it begins to realize it might be construed as offensive. Before then it didn't even think it was offensive, particularly, although some people would construe being beaten to death by a mallet as slightly offensive.

The other element, which is very current in Punch and Judy but which is not often talked about, is the anti-Semitic element. Yes, it creeps in, even into Punch and Judy.[1] It's the presence of pork on the stage. Because, if you remember, they all have endless fights about pork sausages. And in the modern synthetic puppets which people can get off the internet auction houses like eBay and so on, they're made of stringy sort of polystyrene, and they're purple.

They're always fighting. Joey loves the sausages. "*Joey wants the sausages.*" "*No, you're not having them!*" Punch fights with him over the sausages. The Crocodile wants to eat the sausages. The Dragon wants to eat the sausages. The Padre wouldn't mind a few sausages. "*Get up!*" They're all fighting over this meat, essentially, but traditionally real pork was used.

So, the Punchman, or the Professor, had to handle pork, and this meant that it would be an indigenous tradition because a way was found, not entirely consciously, to integrate into it elements which were not for outsiders. This is, in a sense, how folk culture evolves. It implicitly excludes those that it wants to exclude, and that's done quite deliberately.

There are great routines where he wants to turn all the other characters into sausages. He develops a machine, and he puts it on the stage. The policeman comes up then. "*Hello! What are you*

---

[1] To a questioner who asks if anti-Semitism is the reason Punch has a big nose, Bowden replies, "That's an attenuated sublimation of the same thing."

doing?" He wants to turn Joey into a sausage. He wants to turn Scaramouche into a sausage. He wants to turn everyone else into a sausage. The Crocodile comes up and wants to eat them.

There's all sorts of jiggery-pokery with pans, because you cook the sausages in a pan, and somebody grabs the pan and belts them, and they go down again and come up behind. And if he kills one he feels bad about it, but he doesn't really. *"I haven't got a conscience!"* And they all scream, *"You haven't got a conscience!?"* Then he screams, *"Liars! Liars!"* and this sort of thing. It's quite fun. The Skeleton comes up again and doesn't speak. The Bottler says, *"Ooooaaah! The Skeleton! There he is!"* And he goes down again to be replaced by the Devil, and so on.

Other characters include the Hobby-Horse. The idea in popular diction that people ride hobby-horses when they've got a bit of particular enthusiasm of one form or another. Punch gets on his horse and rides, rides, rides and runs to one side. Then he's a bit bored. He turns around and rides to the other side. Then Hobby-Horse disappears.

Another character is the Doctor. Doctors have been hated down the ages by everybody, and this is a chance for the audience to describe how they dislike the doctor. The Doctor appears with a starch-white collar and an enormous moustache, and he's bald and quite posh and snobby. The Doctor appears and says, *"Hello, my boy, in again?"* The Doctor is a complete quack who will be beaten by Punch mercilessly. But, of course, he's got a lotion called Physick. *"What you need, m'boy, is some Physick. Physick is what you need."* Because they've all been beaten up, you see. So, what they need is some snake-oil, basically. Because he's a snake-oil salesmen. The Doctor is told, *"Shut up, you quack!"* Punch is always beating him. *"Oh, hitting a man of the cloth! Hitting a man of the medical profession!"* He goes down again and another one comes up.

Now, there's always retribution for Punch's transgressive amoralism, and the retribution is in the form of the law and the state. The Policeman is one. *"Hello, Hello, Hello! What have you been doing? You've thrown out your baby. You've thrown out your wife. You've beaten the Crocodile to death. You reprobate, reprobate! You need to be 'anged!"* And Punch is deaf, you see, because he's old. He always says, "*I don't want to be fanged.*" "*No, 'anged!*" "*Spanked?*" "*No! 'Anged, boy. You're going to be 'anged, you understand? You're going to take some rope.*" Says the Policeman over here. And Punch says, "*I don't want any hope! I don't need any soap!*" "*No,*" he says "*rope! Rope!*" And the children are howling because of all these lexicographical and grammatical and verbal mistakes that Punch knows full well, because he's dragging out the moment when he's going to be hanged.

The traditional way in which he's going to be hanged involves a whole miscellany of characters, some of whom appear or not. Sometimes they're just melded into one. There's the Hangman or the Executioner who has a hood over his head and he's often called Jack Ketch, who was a very famous executioner at the beginning of the 18th century. Indeed, when the body was thrown to him people in the audience would say "*Ketch that, me old son!*" Because Ketch is a catcher. He often throws the Baby to Ketch saying, "*Get a load of that, mate!*" He gets hold of it and goes down at one end of the stage and then pops up again.

The other figure of amusement/contempt/state power is the Beadle. The Beadle, whose figure has sort of died out in English life, was traditionally a figure that imposes parish law on behalf of a rather faceless magistrate in the neighboring town. The Beadle, or as Punch calls him, "*the Black Beetle!*" "*Don't call me that! Don't call me that! Have you no respect for a man of the law!?,*" directs the gibbet upon which Punch is going to be hanged for his many, many infractions which are almost too numerous to mention, including beating the Devil to death, but we'll come on to that a bit later.

The building of the gibbet is very important, though it's usually just a noose in the middle of the yellow and red stage. Sometimes the Judge is involved, the Beadle's involved, the Hangman's involved, the Policeman's involved, and they're all building it. Punch says, "*I don't understand how you are to be hanged.*" And he gets him to illustrate how he's going to be hanged, which is how he traps them.

In a very famous, world famous, *Punch and Judy* skit or performance within the drama, the Beadle says, "*You mean you've lived for several centuries and you don't know how to be 'anged?*" And he says, "*That's right! I don't know. I haven't mastered the gist of it. You tell me. How are you to be hanged?*" And the Beadle says, "*Well, it's only for illustrational purposes, and children don't do this at home . . .*" And the Bottler shouts, "*Get on with it, you old tart!*" You have all this interactive stuff, all this chat going on at the same time. And the noose is swinging, and this sort of thing.

The Beadle says, "*Well, what you do, old man, is you flex your neck. You need a flexed neck for a good hanging. You need to be in a certain state to be done in properly. Do you know what I mean? Then you put the rope around you. Do you see what I'm doing? Do you want to try it?*" And Punch goes "*Oh, that's very good, very good. I'll give it back to you now.*" The Beadle puts it back on and he says, "*You see, my neck is tensed. It's flexed appropriately.*" The rope's going up and Punch is saying, "*Ah, yes. I see, I see.*" So, you sort of know what's coming.

And then the box comes out. Sometimes there's somebody else, even Pretty Polly or somebody. Somebody "neutral" in a way might come and push the box out. Eventually it builds up, and the children are going absolutely berserk because they adore this sort of thing because it's so asocial and so unmediated and so impolite and so non-adult. And that's why they *adore* it, you see? Because it's also an escapism as well. They know full well what's coming.

The Beadle steps on this box and says, "*Am I doing it correctly?*" "*Yes, Yes! You're doing it really well!*" Eventually, of course, he says, "*Now it's your turn, boy. You're going to be hanged! You're an utter reprobate. You betrayed your wife.*" "*Lies! Lies!*" "*You've thrown your baby out of the window.*" "*Lies! Lies! Lies! You damn liar!*" "*Then you've beaten the law to death!*" "*Lies!*" "*And you've attacked a minister of the cloth!*" "*Lies!*" "*And now you're going to pay! You're going to pay!*"

And Punch comes up behind him and says, "*Like this?*" and he kicks the box away and the Beadle starts to hang like this, "*Oh???! I'm done in, I'm done in, m'love!*" And he's dead. Punch is racing around. "*AHAHAHAHAHA!*" And he laughs for ages! In a chilling sort of a way. And says, "*You're dead! You're dead! You're not red and you've got no cred! And you're really down in the fire! AHAHAHA!*" And all the children are like this, and all the adults are getting slightly nervous, because there is this element of pure power — they're just figurines, you know — that's coming out of the stage. Then there's a sort of resolution, but there isn't.

Now, to get to those moments, because *Punch and Judy* is an improvisatory show, there are lots of gaps and so on. Often, topical figures appear or are introduced. There was one show in Brighton with a well-known Punchman, Byron or one of the others who's well-known, where Saddam Hussein figured, where Osama bin Laden figured once, but that was told to be offensive so that had to be changed. Because, of course, these are just figures against whom we spit and throw potatoes and that sort of thing, you know. They're just sort of mob "we're against them" figures. Occasionally, Alex Ferguson's head will appear, and people will hiss and boo and throw stuff at it. This sort of thing is integrated. Anything can be introduced. Tony Blair was introduced and people were howling outrage: "Death to Blair!" The noose comes down, and everyone cheers. Then it is replaced by someone else.

Some of the most famous skits are the following: the thing begins, and Punch comes on from the right side, and it begins quite slowly. "*Hello! Hello, boys and girls!*" It begins quite slowly, and then Judy appears. "*Oh god . . . Hello.*" "*Hello, darling.*" She produces the Baby. The Baby appears in the middle of them as this stick. Punch initially likes the Baby. "*Oh, so nice. Yes, lovely, lovely.*" Then the Baby starts crying. "*Wah! Wah!*" And Punch goes, "*Shut up. Shut up!*" And it gets worse. She's going, "*Soothe the Baby.*" He says, "*I'll take the Baby.*" And he starts massaging the Baby with his club around the head going, "*Ah, tickery-dock. Oh, lovely baby. Lovely baby.*" The Baby's going, "*WAH! WAH!*" Punch says, "*SHUT UP! God, you're so ugly! Did I really bear YOU!?*" "*Of course, my sweet!*" she says from the side.

In the end, the Baby screams so much and becomes so angry and livid, which is the Punchman doing it from underneath where the puppets are, that Punch gets . . . *transgressive*. He starts to indicate that he's going to throw the Baby into the audience. He goes, "*ONE, TWO, THREE . . .*" and people are going "*No! Don't do it!*" and others are going, "*Go ahead, boy!*" The Bottler's going, "*Now now, is he going to throw it, children? Is he going*

The Real Meaning of Punch & Judy 151

to do it? Is he going to do it!? My god!" Some say, *"Yes! Yes!"* and some go, *"No! No!"* In the end, he throws it right into the audience! Judy goes *"aahhh"* and almost collapses down because she's on this side and the Professor drops her down. Punch is there and capers about like a madman. *"AHAHAHA! No more trouble with that one!"*

Suddenly, the Skeleton appears, his conscience. The Bottler goes, *"Ooooh! Ooooh! There he is!"* He's there, but Punch can't see it, because he hasn't got a conscience. But he's worried by the presence of this numinous force, this slightly metaphysical idea, his conscience which he hasn't got. So, he runs about trying to find his conscience, because if you've lost it you need to find it, don't you? So, he's trying to get it back. *"Where have you gone, then?"* He looks, and then the Skeleton can come down again to be replaced by Joey.

Everyone loves Joey, you see, because it's Punch without any malevolence, which is why Punch can never destroy him. But he's very irritating, Joey. He's always going, *"Mmm hmmm hmm."* And doing little experiments and little tricks. Punch goes, *"God, you're so boring! I want to beat you to death!"* Which is the response to a bad and tedious vaudeville turn. So, Joey always escapes and always manages to get away and usually reappears with sausages, which Punch adores. Punch goes, *"Ah, sausages!"* They follow each other around, and a little hob comes up, and he's put on a little tray, and there's a little platform outside the base of the stage. Punch is looking over, and the sausages are sizzling. The Minister comes along and says, *"You wouldn't give me one of those out of Christian charity?"* and Punch says, *"No!"* and hits him in the head, and he disappears again.

Various other characters come up again. The Crocodile appears because the Crocodile is drawn by the sausages. Now, whenever I have performed *Punch and Judy* with the puppets for children and adults, children of all ages, I always configure the Crocodile with an Ulster accent. I don't know why. But I think he should have an Ulster accent, you know what I mean? *"I want those wee porkers! I want 'em, and I bloody well better have 'em! You know what I mean? Heh? Heh? You know what I mean?"* He comes up like this and Punch says, *"You Irish buffoon!"* and tries to brain him, basically. And the Crocodile says, "*I'm not havin' any o' that! Takin' abuse from a wife-batterer is a step I can't tolerate!*"

And he eats Punch! He eats Punch. He eats his head. His mouth comes around his neck and head and begins to drag him in. Punch is picked up. Sometimes he comes off the puppeteer's hand, which dispels the illusion, but the children, and the adults as well, are so bought into the illusion by that time that these little blips don't matter, because the thing has become magical for them. Punch is going, "*Aaaah! I'm dying! I'm dying!*" and he sort of dies in the Crocodile's mouth. The Crocodile says, "I've done for 'im! They said he couldn't be killed but I've done it, you know?" He takes the sausages and goes down, and the sausages trail along the front of the stage and then whip down.

Then, of course, the Doctor appears. Because when you're dead you need a doctor, don't you? The Doctor appears and says, "*Punch, m'boy, you look a bit piqued, old man, a bit piqued.*" Punch is going, "*I'm deeeead. I'm deeeeeead.*" The Doctor says, "*You don't look too dead to me. You look rather all in.*" "*All in!? You quack!*" The Doctor wants to administer the Physick. He says, "*What you need, Punch, is some Physick. You need some Physick, m'boy. Rub it on your backside, rub it on your spine, rub it under your heart, rub it on your throat, rub it over your brain! Physick in the morning, Physick at tea, Physick in the evening, Physick for me!*" Punch says, "*Shut up, you quack!*" and beats him almost to death, and then he disappears, and the Minister comes up.

He says, "*Oh, Punch! Punch, you've had a near death experience. Has this turned you towards the revelation?*" And Punch says, "*No! Get off, you quack!*" and then the Minister goes back down. The Minister always comes back up and says, "*Dearly beloved, let us sing for Punch, let us pray for Punch and when we are finished . . . buy me a drink.*" Then he goes down again.

Then, of course, it's the Beadle. "*Punch, m'boy! Fighting with crocodiles, stealing sausages, throwing babies, beating your wife to death!*" "*But she's alive! She's alive!*" And then she reappears again. "*Punch, what's happened to the Baby?*" "*Nothing's happened to the Baby.*" "*Has the Crocodile eaten the Baby?*" "*No, no!*"

Because what the Punchman is doing is he's improvising on certain tropes, certain themes, certain set pieces. He's fixed them together in various ways. But the way in which they occur, rather like the way I speak at these meetings, is not predetermined. So, the logic is there, but the way in which it unfolds before you happens heuristically. It happens in the moment. So, it's a sort of existential tradition, but they know where they are going. They know they have these particular set routines, particularly involving the fixed characters: the wife Judy, the mistress Polly.

Polly comes up, and there's Punch leering over the stage like a dirty old man. He comes right over the stage. *"What a package! What a dolly! What a polly, eh?"* But she doesn't speak. He says, *"Speak, me love. Speak words of endearment. Nothing to say?"* She's mute, you see. This is usually slightly excised for the under-fives. She's there, and she's in some ways the motivation to the action. *"What a lovey!"* he says to Polly. *"She's appeared and she's already in love with me! We've only just met!"* Then nemesis, Judy, appears, and he goes, *"Oh, God! It's Judy." "Hello, Punch."* He says, *"What do you want?"* And she says, *"Don't be like that. I've had a hard day."* And then he says, *"What do you mean a hard day!? I've been in the belly of a crocodile and up again! And you say you've had a hard day!"* Then his club comes out, and he wants to beat her to death, and they run around.

These performances go on for 20 minutes, 40 minutes, 45 minutes. The Professor needs a break afterwards, because he's quite exhausted, but it's extraordinarily exhilarating because you give out such power and such energy.

Often, the closure of the piece is the Devil. The Devil comes, again, from the mystery plays and medieval license. Again, he's a sort of figure of nemesis in part to inculcate the idea that Punch is partly heroic when he's actually transgressed against moral norms and against authority and is a showman and a shaman and a trickster and a number one card in the tarot and the one who's always out of step and the one who's cards are thrown on the table. Yet, he's the one who does for the Devil.

The Devil rarely speaks. He's always red with a black cloak and black horns and a hook nose. The Bottler does a lot with the Devil. *"Ooooh there he is! Children, aren't you frightened?"* And they go, "Yes!" and a few brave ones go, "No, no." Punch is wary of the Devil, and then they fall on each other. The Devil sometimes has an axe, and Punch has a club. They're fighting each other. Don't forget that Punch is on the right side. The Devil, spiritually and occultistically, is on the left side. He's sinister. *Sinistere*, you see? The Devil.

They grapple with each other like this, and it gets very violent. It's been known that in their excesses Punchmen have fallen out of the stage in front of everyone, and they gather it together again quickly and keep on. Because the old theatrical adage is "Whatever happens, you keep going." You keep going if one member of the cast dies or has a hallucination. You keep going. There's a famous moment with Olivier at the National when some slightly epicene bloke falls off the stage and breaks his leg. Breaks his leg! Crack! There's whole silence in the theater, and the director says get back on, and he's made to crawl up back onto the stage. So, all forms of life have their courage, you see. This is the form it takes in that area.

Punch and the Devil are fighting each other, and the Devil usually gets the better of Punch. He holds him to the ground and jumps on top of him. Because, say Punch is down here and the Professor's hand is inside him, and the Devil gets on top of him and leaps on down. The Bottler provides the verbal amphitheater. Then Punch throws him off with a Herculean burst that Dr. Johnson would have approved of. Johnson, when asked, said "the first Whig was the devil." Whig, of course, was a term for liberal in that era.

Eventually, Punch gets on top of the Devil and beats him, beats him very severely. He beats him down to the ground. The Devil gets up again and throws him off. He's down on the stage. The Devil leaps on top of him. Punch gets more and more strong. The Right seems to dominate the Left more and more. The Devil squirms and gets to the side, dancing back. He gets on top of him. He beats him. He starts leaping and whooping and that sort of thing. And eventually the Devil dies and expires.

The Bottler comes out from around the back and goes, "*Children, lords and ladies, moms and dads! The Devil is dead! The Devil is dead! And the man who's done it, I give it to you, is Mr. Punch!*" He takes a bow for killing the Devil. He goes, "*Thank you! Thank you, very much! Thank you! Nine to five . . .*" The Devil's lying there, and this is an amazing moment.

For many years the Church used to try and ban these performances because they're often performed outside mass, often performed outside in the churchyard, and they try to move it into secular ground. Too many people were coming directly out of church and watching this ribald and/or other entertainment.

He leaps on top of the Devil and screams, "*The Devil is dead! The Devil is dead! And now you're free to do what you want!*" Which is quite the transgressive idea, of course. This is an under-five audience, you know.

Then he dips down. Usually, there's a side interlude bit of music. The Bottler gets the trumpet out, which of course is a punctuation device. It's a way of slowing the action, because you build people up and then you let them go, and then you build them up again. Then you usually go to the sequences with is the gibbet, which is the attempt at closure.

Then after it's all over, of course, the curtains on the front of the stage go across. It's just on a switch, and you whip them across. Smaller versions of the red and yellow awning that go from the top to the bottom. There's enormous applause because usually, if the Punchman's any good, if the Professor can do it, you can hold children because of the ferocity and the primal nature of it. It's designed at every moment never to be boring.

It's a type of pure cardinal performance. It's not intellectual at all. It's completely unmediated. The energy comes straight out of the performer, it comes into the audience, and he rips it back out again. They give a lot of energy that he also recycles to them.

It's pure theater. The people who see it when they are very young, particularly the very violent dolls, the very Victorian ones with heavy *papier-mâché* heads, so every time Punch hits them or brains them you hear the bang, you hear the clunk. Clunk, clunk! It's quite physical, quite animalian, and also slightly animist.

I know there was a famous modern Punchman from Bolton who would never allow his characters to be hanged. When somebody asked why he said, "Because they're alive!" There is this streak in all of these performance related arts (ventriloquism is the most famous) where they do take on a life of their own.

I knew a ventriloquist, and the doll would be in the corner of the room. The doll would have gray skin and these big red rubbery lips. The doll was completely hideous, and had long nails. It had a sort of fonteral suit with a bow tie and a striped waistcoat.

The doll is the unconscious of the performer, or semi-consciousness of the performer. So, you say, "Hello, Robert." And it would say, *"Oh, God! That bastard's turned up."* And he'd say "Shut up! Shut up!" because the negative side, the *anima* in Jungian terms, would come out of the doll. It would say, *"He doesn't like you, you know."* The ventriloquist says, "Shut up! He's such a bad boy." Because the negative element of the personality comes out of the doll.

There's a very famous scatological female ventriloquist, and she insults men in the audience. *"Go on, look at him!"* says the doll and that sort of thing. And these blokes, these working class men, they come out and they punch the doll. They punch the doll! Because the doll has insulted them. Because it's alive, you see! It's non-dualist. It's the bit that people don't say to avoid social conflict that comes out through the doll. So, there's always an aggressive sort of tiger-in-the-room element in all of these forms of popular culture. Because they're interactive, they have a dangerous side.

There's no bully, as it were, because in Garrick's day in the 18th century every theater had a bully. You had men at the corner of the stage with clubs. Traditionally, women couldn't be put on the stage because the audience would howl "prostitute!" and this sort of thing. Only at the end of the 19th century with Ellen Terry did it really become respectable for a woman to be on the stage. Many men, if they saw a woman on the stage, would immediately think she was available. So, they would get on the stage and leap towards her. So Garrick would whistle, and a bully would come out of the wing and get hold of the reprobate, flog him, and drag him out into the strand or drag him out into Charing Cross Road, where the Garrick Theater now is, and throw him into the dirt. And Mrs. Defrelli or whoever it is would rearrange her bodice and continue the performance. Always a trooper, you see.

That type of energy is dimmed by television, dimmed by the collapse of vaudeville in our culture in the 1950s. How many of you have seen *The Entertainer* by John Osborne with Olivier, when at the end there's only three old beers at the back of the audience, the music hall is dying in the '50's and Olivier says, "*I'm dead, you know, loves. Dead behind the eyes*"? And one of the old beers at the back says, "God, this isn't much fun, is it?"

But *Punch and Judy* is a lot more fun and a lot more grotesque and quite dangerous actually. The endless prohibitions which have been put on it, church prohibitions, liberal, state, and materialist prohibitions, entertainment license prohibitions. You don't see it very much at the seaside now.

But it's sort of been morphed and resurrected as a cardinal folk tradition, usually with the racial and pork sausage element played down and the sexual dimension with the mistress Polly of course played down. But still, that cardinal element.

The modernist composer Harrison Birtwistle wrote an opera called *Punch and Judy*, and Stephen Pruslin wrote the libretto. It was his first piece, and it's a very violent expressionistic piece in many ways.

Most of the traditional Punchmen don't like Glyn Edwards and Michael Byrom and George Speaight, who wrote the cultural history of *Punch and Judy* that came out about 35 years ago, and certain others. Geoff Felix is a well-known Punchman and wrote a book of recollections which consists of them all talking about their lives and this sort of thing.

Many of them led fascinating lives. Traditionally, they would just go about in a car. They had no home. Their home was the next tent. Their home was the next performance. They lived on what they got in the bottle. Traditionally, they're called Bottlers because you go around with a bottle at the end, and people put coins in it. "*Some money! Some money for your man! The money for the performer!*" And everyone is just putting in some coins. At the end of it, we're talking about pre-modern money of course, it would be filled to the lip, and you would smash the bottle in front of the audience and all the coins would go all over, but you'd have the Bottler to get them up quickly because that's what you needed to live on until the next performance. Now that won't work because you can't live on 320 a week, which is what coppers filling a bottle would amount to. But people throw fivers and so on.

What they do now is children's parties. Where, in a way, the tradition is castrated and slightly emasculated. It's too twee. It's too polite. It's too likeably nice. And it's too small. In the average living room, the energy that's created by this very macabre theater is too small. But I personally think that Punch and Judy is an extraordinary example of the folk tradition.

It always makes me smile that you have major cultural Marxists like Theodor Adorno, who wrote an enormous 800-page book in the middle of the 20th century called *Aesthetic Theory* which is the basis of quite a lot of ideas about contemporary culture. And they dislike the cultural industry. They dislike the industry that provides Madonna and Michael Jackson as the colophons, as the icons, which you are drawn to adore. The Amy Winehouse types. He dislikes all of that.

Yet, if you follow through the logic of what Adorno is saying, one of his criticisms must be that it's transplanted these folkish forms. That it has transplanted these organic forms. That it's pushed them to the side. But in all truth, he wouldn't like many of these organic forms in their fauna and flora, and in their violence and amorality, in their textural lividness, in their Greek tragedy without necessarily the hard words and concepts.

It's called *The Tragicomedy of Punch and Judy,* and the best theaters, the very large 19th century ones which were very elaborate, had the theatric figures of tragedy (misery) and comedy (humor). Because one moment he's crying and the next moment he's beating them to death. Enjoying himself, in other words. Leaping on the Devil, you know. Wouldn't you like to leap on the Devil? It goes from comedy to tragedy to tragicomedy to burlesque to sentimentality and back again. Popular culture like this really has two nodal points. Sort of aggression and sentimentality, in a way.

But the speed with which they interchange with each other can be quite profound and quite liberating for an audience. It often exhausts an audience. The audience is often exhausted at the end of it. They've been to a rally. They've been to the equivalent of a political rally and yet receive no ideology. That's the trick of that type of performance.

Although it's a distant point, you can say that politicians and people who attempt to influence society . . . I mean, no academic would give a performance like that, would they? It's contraindicated. You can't do it. Because it's a sort of carnal type of culture. You're actually giving a physiological performance. The words are largely noises. Which is why Punch is always making noises.

One point I haven't made is that the Punchman has a device in his mouth called a swazzle through which he creates this sound. You can create it without that, of course, but the tradition is you have this thing in your mouth. This is quite difficult because you have to have it on a chain or a bit of rope. Because when the swazzle's in your mouth you're going, but when another character comes you have to spit the swazzle out and speak more normally, like the Policeman.

I think there is a parallel to be drawn between certain types of extremist political speaking and these types of performances. Because that type of speaking, which is now completely disprivileged in current political discourse, involves speaking to the *whole* audience. It involves speaking to the front of the brain, to the back of the brain. It involves speaking intellectually but also cardinally, also semi-carnally. It involves taking energy from the audience and giving it back. It's partly a theatrical performance as well as an ideological and semi-intellectual one.

It's deeply disprivileged now. Hardly any politician can do it. The type of performance that is permitted now is Obama's. Where Obama has a device here and a device there, and he looks at the one, and he looks at the other, and he says, "Today . . . in America . . . we are born . . . for the greatness . . . which is coming." And he gives a very big grin. The teleprompter gives the words, and it's all in about 20 or 18 points. The size of it is enormous.

Indeed, Bush II was so thick that the teleprompters would often have false words because he might get confused if they were properly spelled. So, he had to have these false words like "desert" would be "dezurt" or something just to get his mouth around it. It needed to be phonetic, so he could grasp it and not say "Gee, what's that?" in the middle of it, with the whole media watching him. "These . . . terrorists . . . that . . . we . . . need . . . to . . . pun-ish." Like Gerry Adams' Gaelic. Have you ever heard Gerry Adams speak Gaelic? His political use of language. He speaks Gaelic like this: [halting, choppy, unintelligible]. "John said I'm a man." It's a political use of language.

Because if you speak too aggressively, too unselfconsciously, too much with a theatrical flow, it's regarded as fascistic. I remember David Owen once—and David is a very poor speaker, sort of a paint drying sort of a chap—but he always used to address his Social Democratic Party, that tiny little party that split away even from the SDLP [Social Democratic and Labour Party of Northern Ireland], if you remember all that bother about 20 years ago. He used to address them in a slightly authoritarian way. He'd be in black. They'd be down there. He'd be up there. People talked about the new Caesarism. I mean David Owen!

But even something like that, which was not trying to befriend the audience, which was not feeling the audience's pain, which is the Blair and Clinton thing. "I feel your pain. I feel your pain." You're reaching out into the audience. It's sort of a lie. Of course it's a lie. It's a sort of therapeutic discourse rather than a militaristic one.

Do you think Julius Caesar in front of the legions would have spoken like that? Do you think Napoleon would have spoken like that? Do you think even Ulysses S. Grant, if you like, would have spoken like that? Or leaders on the Confederate side? Do you think Montgomery could have addressed the 8th Army like this? You know, reach out to the tankman and say, "I feel your pain."

When you realize that the discourse shapes the nature of the society and shapes the nature of the minds of the people in the society. If you say, "I'm sorry. You're going to get old; you're going to die. I'm so, so, so sorry." What sort of a society will you have if this isn't your last word but your first! Your *first* word when you go to a mass audience.

The important thing about public speaking is never to be afraid. The second important thing is never to give a damn. And that means you can just get up in front of people. The third thing, which is an old actor's technique, is you must never be frightened of making a fool of yourself. In actor's college, you go on, and they all laugh at you: "Look at that idiot!" They almost throw things at you. You imagine breaking your leg on stage. Once you've made a mistake you're less afraid about making another one because you just step over the prospect that you might make one.

Another trick to all real performance is *domination of the audience*. You have to be up there, and they're looking at you. All rock stars and all these other people use some of these techniques because they've gone into those areas. They're not allowed militarily too much. They're not allowed at all politically because then they may be authoritarian. So they've gone into other areas. You can never destroy anything. You can just displace it. Usually to some internet site they haven't taken down yet.

But there is a degree to which these sort of techniques are very, very useful. Particularly in a democratic age, because you can speak to 40 and speak to three million using the internet as the weapon to do so. The irony is, you see, in politics you don't speak to people's minds. You speak to them physiologically. You speak to what's *underneath* the mind. Do you think you can raise men up into battle just by talking to what's mentally up here? You influence the brains of the men who will influence them. Your discourse will influence them by doing that, but you don't influence them by doing that.

Tony Blair once said that we went to war in the past between 1914 and 1918 and 1940 and '45 and all the other wars to fight for tolerance. To fight for *inclusion*. Inclusion and tolerance . . . Can you imagine giving your troops a bit of tolerance and inclusion before they went over the top!? Of course not! You give them something quite different. Quite different! Almost totally unrepeatable in a way, and probably the men in the back couldn't quite hear what the bloke was saying anyway, but they understood what it meant.

You see, real speaking, they understand what you mean even if they don't understand what you *say*! Because it is the way in which you say it, and the energy which goes into certain subconscious parts of the brain. Of course, there was a man who came earlier in the 20th century who had a very considerable talent for this type of speaking. He was regarded as very dangerous. But all sorts of other people have had that talent, which is inborn. It can be trained. You can make people better, but in the end it's inborn. It's a way in which you can mobilize very large numbers of people. The question is, "For what?" And why will they follow?

A critic would put his hand up and say, "What you're saying is all very well, but why would they follow your discourse rather than another?" My view is this: if you speak as in these puppeteering performances, from a position which is primal, from a position which is organic, from a position that comes out of the ground and relates to the corpses and the genealogies of that which was before you, you can make mistakes, you can abstract things, you can go on to different parts, but the audience understands where you are coming from, because they hear the echoes of the voices that have spoken before you. And that is why they respond in that physical way.

Newton, the scientist, was an incredibly arrogant, slightly sociopathic, and quite unpleasant man, but he was once asked, "How did you come across the second law of thermodynamics?" Newton, in physics, discovered the idea that energy in a system always replaces itself when it's used. Now, Newton said something very interesting for a man who was so full of himself, and so full of *hubris* as the Greeks would have said. He said, "I saw further than the others because I stood on the shoulders of giants."

And that is why you can influence an audience. Because they know what existed before you, and you are basically plugging in. You are putting the plug in the socket, and you are turning the switch down. Nietzsche, in one of his books, in *Will to Power* and in others, the notebooks collected after his death by his sister, says, "Not me. Not me, but the wind that flows through me." It's the idea that when you're in such a mode certain things flow through you from the past, from what is rooted, from which is underneath you. And it can affect people. It can . . . liberate is the wrong word, can *free* elements of the mind that are otherwise restricted. It can get them to see the truth about life.

That's why there's this odd interconnection between high and low forms of culture, because the high intellectualizes the primal energy of the low. As soon as you begin to theorize or philosophize about the motivations of these sorts of characters, even though they're made of wood and *papier-mâché*, you immediately have tragedy. Because if you begin to understand the motivations of the method of destruction you're immediately dealing with the questions of Aeschylus' *Oresteia*. You leap from the very low, if it's organic and rooted, to the very high, and can go back again.

This is why liberal society is cancerous, ultimately, of real culture because it divides the interconnectedness between the high and the low and prevents the energy coming up from beneath, from the bottom to the top. A real culture has everyone involved in the culture, not watching the idiocy of Ferguson's latest team of foreign imports, but understanding the nature of their own culture, from top to bottom. In Shakespeare's day, the whole society was in the theater, the lower class, the middling class, the upper class. They were all there.

All the sword fights and the extreme switches of scenery and the instantaneous scenes that suddenly they're full of language but they shift and they're very quick. That's to keep it going so people won't get bored. The Jester. The fool in *Lear*. And if they were bored, they would throw fruit and nuts out of the pit at the actors, and they'd realize that they had to speed things up.

Henry Irving in the 19th century was very funny. (Whether Henry Irving and David Irving are at all related I've got no idea.) Henry Irving is the greatest actor of late Victorian England. Always played monsters. Always played Mephistopheles. Always played these sorts of characters. But when he would forget the lines, he would make it up, because he was such a so-and-so.

If he was on the heath doing *Lear*, you know: "Ho, bloody beadle! Why dost thou whip that whore? Thy lust is so used up for that kind for which thou whipped her," which is a couple of stanzas from *Lear*. If he can't remember the next bit he'll just go, "And as the owls do breach the lofty turns, this tree a storm!"

which he's just made up. Because you've got to have that sort of facility to continue it.

There's somebody in the wings desperately trying to get a message across to you as to what you should be saying. Of course, that's why the wings are there. Because when you forget your part the man's got to go "No! no!" and try and give you a bit of it. The theatrical dimension, the excitement . . .

Think how exciting those political meetings would have been before television. Think how innovating and energizing they would be. After one of those sorts of meetings you'd want to take your entire society over, wouldn't you? Rather than just go back and watch *The X Factor* on the box. You would feel invigorated and empowered. That's the purpose of these. They're almost like secular religious events. That's what these forms of culture are, and that is why they're not liked, and that is why they're slightly disprivileged, and that is why they are scorned. If you want to win a battle in a court you don't speak in this way, but if you wish to take a society back, you take some cognizance of these traditional forms.

Thank you very much!

Counter-Currents/*North American New Right*
January 17, 2011

WHY I WRITE

This is always difficult to assess, but from this distance three different spear-points become discernible through the mist.

The first is an obvious desire for self-expression—yet, as always, the nihilism of Samuel Beckett needs to be avoided, where, during one part of the *Trilogy*, such as *Molloy*, he declares: nothing to express, no need to express, a blinding desire to stain the silence. I think that the *aporia* whereby postmodernism eats itself needs to be avoided.

Nonetheless, I believe that fantasy or the phantasia of the semi-conscious mind is the most important vector, aesthetically speaking. All of my fictional work comes out of the *anima* or that part of consciousness just beneath rationality. All of my texts—like *Kratos* or *The Fanatical Pursuit of Purity*, for example—are dreams.

But dreaming to what end? Well, the essential starting point is a desire to overcome dualism in the ethical sense. This imputes the following: that all of my characters, in a short story like "Origami Bluebeard," are neither good nor evil. They are—more fundamentally—a mixture of both, and they feed upon each other like raptors within a world of the uncouth.

Nor is this a purely misanthropic vision either, in that heroic vigor is just the flip side of negativism. Character, at least as posited in these stories, is biological, prior ordained, morphic, and predestined—it is primarily Augustinian in theological terms, in other words. But contrary to most Judeo-Christian estimations of *Kultur*, this is not observed in a woe-begotten or morbid state. Instead of these dark threnodies, the heathen logic of Robert E. Howard is more applicable. The current estimation is very much that civilization and barbarism are mutually exclusive, but I believe that you cannot have the one without the other.

In these stories, plays, novellas, and novels—even the non-fiction dialogue, *Apocalypse TV*—I have attempted to overcome dualism within a non-humanist motif. This means that the characters are dolls or puppets in terms of Artaud's Theatre of Cruelty, at one level, but they are also much more alive at another. In most contemporary liberal novels—Iris Murdoch's *The Philosopher's Pupil* by illustration—only the villainous, macabre, or negative specimens have life. Whereas in my efforts—such as a tragic story like *Napalm Blonde*—all of the characters bite and rage; love is voltaic, unpronounced, and beyond the remit of good and evil.

Why is this done? Merely to provide a template whereby the battle occurs betwixt the superhuman and the subhuman, *per se*, and it exists across or between individuals. My view is that immersion in dreamlike or solipsistic material that has a different rhythm or vibration will turn Caucasian wimps into cultured Neanderthals. For what is required is an attitude to life which goes forward towards the great noontide, open-armed, in the manner of the sun-worship at the end of Hermann Hesse's *The Glass Bead Game*.

I am not preaching anti-intellectuality, but extolling the licentiousness and chthonian violence of reintegration. The affliction which Indo-Europeans suffer from is entirely mental and subjective; they are chronically afraid of their own shadow, in Jungian terms. If the civilization which their ancestors created has any future at all then they must overcome their resistance to barbarism; they must o'erleap it on the altar of high culture. They must dispel the cloud and lay out a future where Arthur Butz's credo doesn't have to be true (or not).

Truthfully, in this age those with intellect have no courage and those with some modicum of physical courage have no intellect. If things are to alter during the next 50 years then we must re-embrace Byron's ideal: the cultured thug.

Counter-Currents/*North American New Right*
August 18, 2010

JONATHAN BOWDEN'S
APOCALYPSE TV

Jonathan Bowden
Apocalypse TV
London: The Spinning Top Club, 2007

Apocalypse TV was published in August 2007 by the Spinning Top Club. It runs to 239 pages and contains a pencil sketch of the author in the frontispiece or prelims by Michael Woodbridge. It is quite different to the other books which I have reviewed by this author—novels and plays, etc.—by being directly non-fictional in character.

Yet, on closer examination, I wonder if the author really thinks this. For, like Nietzsche, I believe that he scorns academic specialization into different, diffuse, finite, and often trivial disciplines. Didn't Nietzsche's *Birth of Tragedy* virtually finish off philology at a stroke?

Also, and more importantly, Bowden follows Bill Hopkins here, in that he believes overspecialization led to a corresponding primitivism at the end of the 19th century. This was partly a result of whey-faced specialism—an absence of fury—and it led to an expressive interest in primitive culture outside Europe . . . partly as a response. I think that both Bowden and Hopkins in no sense disprivilege the primeval, but they prefer it to come from within Nation Europa by virtue of the Cycladic culture in archaic Greece, say.

Nonetheless, *Apocalypse TV* is a Platonic dialogue of metapolitical import. It consists of two independent voices which both appear to be "hardline" and illiberal in tone. They are also highly educated and cultivated—yet, in this context, cultural knowledge does not presuppose a weak or milksop attitude. I believe that this text appeared for a brief period on the British National Party website when the author was that group's unpaid cultural officer between May 2004 and August 2007. I understand that he is no longer associated with that political party whatsoever. He is now Chairman of a philosophical group called the British New Right which spreads elitist and non-humanist ideas.

One of the characters or *dramatis personae* in this dialogue is a Nietzschean (Frederick) and the other an avowed Christian (Thomas). These two puppets or stage-maneuvered characters are obviously stand-ins for Nietzsche and Thomas Aquinas, respectively. Yet there is no attempt at an easy way out here — since both characters are anti-liberal in a very radical or fanatical way. The Judeo-Christian voice is almost on a par with the theodicy of Mel Gibson's traditionalist film *The Passion of the Christ*.

This means that both voices are virtually as Right-wing as each other. The physical-cum-textual dialogue is split about 50/50 between them. Neither voice really wins, and they often agree, but Bowden's preference for the pagan and vitalist voice is implicitly obvious. Likewise, a clash between metaphysical subjectivisms and objectivisms occurs herein.

These two dynamic wills debate political correctness as a grammar of modernity, radical modernist art *à la* the Brit or anti-objectivist tendency in Britain, mass migration, the politics of the liberal European Union, contemporary (then) Blairite politics in the UK, popular delusions and mass media inanity, as well as criminology. A very detailed, factual, and yet immediate narrative follows on from this. A humorous element amidst the disputation of these two (quite rare in this type of material) is also discernible.

One thing stands out to me, withal, and this is the originality of the approach as well as the range of cultural knowledge evinced. There is a striking subtext of factual accuracy which is quite rare in works that are propagandistic in intent. Similarly, on the EU the hard or fascistic notion of integration is discussed (never looked at in contemporary Euro-babble); while phenomena such as the U.S. militia movement and the activities of the Unabomber are mulled over. The analysis is slightly dated due to the fact that the dialogues appear to have taken place in the late '90s or thereafter. The attentive reader just substitutes present synonyms for proper names like Clinton, Bush, Blair, Gorbachev, Mitterrand, Yeltsin, etc.

The only glaring omission is the relative absence of Islam throughout the text. Indeed, the Christian personification (Thomas) mentions this at one point. Quite clearly, this text originated and was edited before the Twin Towers and the unfolding events that came after it. Other than that, it proves how little the core issues have changed after more than a decade.

Two areas stand out for this reviewer. The first is the dialogue called "Sex, Death, Fred and Rose." This is a duologue (Aeschylus' invention in theater) over a notorious married couple who were sadistic erotic killers. They were known as Fred and Rose West. I suppose comparable American cases in your criminology and penology would be the Bundy affair, Son of Sam, the Tate-LaBianca murders, and the Leopold and Loeb cases. (The latter was filmed by Alfred Hitchcock in *Rope*.)

It's a fascinating dialogue because the Christian tends to think that such individuals are possessed *à la* Dostoyevsky's novel; the pagan (Frederick) mulls over this case existentially. But only in part—since, although his locution is much closer to Camus or Dürrenmatt, Fred believes that biology and Krafft-Ebing's *Psychopathia Sexualis* plays a much more blatant role.

The other very interesting dialogue is over Modern art— where the anti-objectivist Turner Prize is considered from every angle. Interestingly, the author has the Christian adopt a more aesthetically conservative and "reactive" point of view — whereas the Nietzsche substitute seems to be much more sympathetic to the extremely imaginary, but not in every case.

Stewart Home's book about postmodern art and other marginals, *The Assault on Culture*, is also analyzed by our twosome. This consists of fringe art movements like Situationism, Fluxus, Lettrism, the Movement for an Imagist Bauhaus, Auto-Destructive art, etc. . . . yet the far-Left, materialist and ideologically "neo-proletarian" prefix often falls sheer. Since, in Home's very description, Mail Art involves an artist sending, unsolicited, various representational paintings of Adolf Hitler to all sorts of people who probably didn't wish to be in receipt.

(Bowden's antennae were very acute here. When *Apocalypse*

TV was composed Home was a very minor player. But after this he has emerged as the writer-in-residence at the Tate Gallery in London. Jonathan Bowden has also devoted an oration or talk on this area called "Stewart Home and Cultural Communism." It can be found on YouTube.[1])

All in all, this philosophical dialogue harks back to one of the West's oldest forms—namely, a debate between two lively minds. It also hints that both pagans and Christians are going to have to collaborate (up to a point) in the cultural war. Indeed, the only real source of tension between these dual personifications involves *ethics*. Perhaps the author is hinting that Western culture is a Christian-pagan hybrid—just like Evola who always described his faith system as Catholic-pagan. (Note: The Paganism he's referring to relates to the ancient world.) I have to say that every radical Right point of interest, intersection, and debate is dealt with in this volume. Tens of thousands of *Apocalypse TV* have been disseminated, but its themes are not just restricted to the British Isles.

I will close this review with the following remark. Two writers who were members of the Angry Young Men in the '50s, Bill Hopkins and Colin Wilson, used to have debates with one another that lasted around 17 hours. Each would sit back-to-back on wooden stools in a bare or semi-deserted room. Some of this was recollected in Wilson's books about '50s Soho.

Nevertheless, this is genuine dialectic—it is high Western intellect, where each intellectual is given a space to articulate a viewpoint, to think aloud, without interruption. Then his colleague has to take up the tennis racket in the match. There are no political correctnesses, no false boundaries, no unsayable propositions (even on one's own side). There remain no boundaries to pure thinking. This is presently what all Western universities or tertiary institutions of learning lack. Yet if it isn't allowed in the Ivy League it will gravitate elsewhere . . . some call it detribalization amongst intellectuals; it is probably the only way in which you could transform a carpet-bagging liberal into a cultural fundamentalist.

---

[1] http://www.youtube.com/watch?v=S8tjGJ4eUdA

It is the nearest thing you will ever get to the debates between the philosophers in Ancient Greece—yet it hails from a primordial standpoint.

John Michael McCloughlin
Counter-Currents/*North American New Right*
October 31, 2010

JONATHAN BOWDEN'S
AL-QA'EDA MOTH

Jonathan Bowden
Al-Qa'eda MOTH
London: The Spinning Top Club, 2008

This picaresque novel was published in August 2008 by the Spinning Top Club in England. The novel is a slightly unusual departure for Bowden in that it is a Western—albeit of a spectral or ghoulish sort. It could be best described as a supernatural Western crossed with an intellectual treatise.

It is interesting to note that the literary Western is customarily despised, and, unlike its film variant, there is very little "serious" criticism devoted to it. Although some of the most famous practitioners of this area—Zane Grey, Louis L'Amour, and Elmore Leonard—are obviously well-known (Grey's total sales exceed 250 million copies), the area as a whole receives scant respect. Whether or not this is because Francis Parker Yockey's Hero of the Second World War's favorite author was Zane Grey in translation is a moot point.

To date, Bowden has only written one Western, and the title itself is intriguing. From what I can work out having read the book several times it appears to mean exploding moths or insects—it definitely has nothing to do with Islamism whatsoever. On reflection, the title may relate to his old friend the anti-humanist intellectual Bill Hopkins. In an interview between them in the late '90s, Hopkins confirmed that he was writing a play called *Phosphorescent Insects* about animal liberation. I think it was to be the *sine qua non* of misanthropy—the insects in question, entropically, being Mankind—but Hopkins never finished it to his satisfaction after three drafts. My belief is that Bowden has always specialized in insects—*A Ballet of Wasps*, etc.—and he wanted to use the idea of Lepidoptera speeding rapidly around their extinguishment, in fire, as his motif.

The book itself involves three distinct storylines which overlap with each other in a way that takes the Western into undeveloped territory. Bowden's thesis is why not use a form some consider hackneyed to analyze the West, the Occident, or the remains of the civilization we could be said to be living in. To this end, and in a manner that's confirmed by the book's blurb, volumes like Lawrence R. Brown's *The Might of the West* and William Gayley Simpson's *Which Way Western Man?* are used as templates or sounding-boards for the narrative.

Bowden wants to discuss whether Western culture has a future, and he does so by assessing five centuries of Western painting since the Renaissance. This happens amid the dream-landscape of the main characters who populate this narrative. The fable (with this exception) is otherwise representational and narrative-driven in its scope. I think that Mister Bowden has chosen the West in an idealized European sense having never been there himself.

California has doubtless changed out of all recognition, but, way back at the beginning of the last century in Robinson Jeffers' poetry, this pellucid West is crying out for tragedy. This happens to be one of the reasons, doubtless, why Jeffers saw the harsh and at that time literally unspoilt wilderness of these great tracks of American land as a vestibule for Tragedy — above all, Greek tragedy. A reason why Jeffers himself went on to conclude a blood-soaked version of Euripides' *Medea* set amidst the immense glare of California's vastness.

In any event, all of the usual Bowden tropes are here — including two parallel narratives involving the same characters or *dramatis personae*. One series of incidents is set in the Old West of the 19th century; the other occurs in the 20th century. The link between the two plot devices is provided by the same personnel in both cases. Bowden also allows himself two violent climaxes — in both storylines — and there is a greater degree of normative good and evil here than usual with him, perhaps influenced by the genre.

The criminal gang (fronted up by Old Man Smithers and his delinquent son Blackbird Leys Dingo) is particularly well-drawn in their baseness. It is a belletristic exercise in insect classification drawn from Jim Dewey's *Deliverance* (from which the famous film was derived) and maybe even the yokel brigands in *Straw Dogs*. Certainly, the analysis here is Lombrosian. Extreme criminality is biological, somatic, genetic, and prior ordained; it can only be faced down by the morality of punishment. There is no hint of Obama's penology here. For, like Robinson Jeffers, the harsh Western sun beats down upon all with a maximal glare and in a fully Pagan transport.

This is the nearest that Jonathan Bowden has ever come to writing a straight adventure story, or series of same, and yet he undercuts this by a dreamy debate about *Kultur*. The West's, that is, and whether the unfulfilled promise of Wyndham Lewis' *The Human Age* trilogy can lead it forwards into aught better.

It is interesting to note that much of the European New Right detests American life so much that they have lost sight of certain verities, but Bowden seeks to reclaim the dissident voices of Mencken, London, Pound, Eliot, Henry Miller's *The Air-Conditioned Nightmare*, the Southern Agrarians, Jeffers, and Revilo P. Oliver. He sees in a dissident, post-Puritan, Apocalyptian, martial-lawed, bleaker, sun-drenched, and full-on Ameri[k]a seeds of a new beginning. It is as if some of the rhetoric of Cotton Mather has displaced itself in time so as to elide with Andrew Macdonald's *Hunter* (the progeny of Doctor Pierce) in order to flower in a violent *Walden*: a parody and Dystopia on the negation of Ellis' *American Psycho*. In any event, the anti-communist, free, wise, and open art of the post-war firmament was abstract expressionism, encoded by Jackson Pollack from small-town Wyoming, and secretly financed by the Central Intelligence Agency. One wonders what they really thought about it all! Nonetheless, isn't it time to put something on the canvas — and yet still remain expressive? Perhaps a skeletal arm, in imagination, reaches out all aflame and surrounded by white sheets . . . in a scenario where Death-on-horseback rides and twists, and where Philip Guston retreats in alarm to from where his later self-portraits originated in Griffith's *Birth of a Nation*.

For those who have ears to hear — let them hear!

John Michael McCloughlin
Counter-Currents/*North American New Right*
October 17, 2010

JONATHAN BOWDEN'S
KRATOS & OTHER WORKS

Jonathan Bowden
Kratos and Other Works
London: The Spinning Top Club, 2008

The book *Kratos* was published by the Spinning Top Club in very early 2008. It extends over 157 pages. It consists of four independent stories of around the same length.

The first ("Kratos") deals with a Lombrosian tale about criminality and *psychopathia*. It delineates a Yorkshire axe-man called Billy-O or Dung Beetle whose intentions are fundamentally misread by an upper-class fop, Basildon Lancaster.

One might characterize it as an exercise in Degeneration theory from the late 19th century brought up to date—hence its debt to Cesare Lombroso's *Criminal Man* from 1876, I believe. A highly filmic coloration befits this piece—almost in a lucid or paranormal light, and this lends it a dreamlike or magical intention. Bowden's pieces tend to be extremely visual, oneiric, outsider-drawn, or filmic in compass—he is definitely what could be called a Visualizer. There also, to this particular critic, seems to be a correlation between all of these fictions and the comics or graphic novels that he produced as a child. All of them have a violent, immediate, and aleatory dimension, to be sure, yet I infer something more.

What I mean is that just like a film which is planned on a storyboard, for example, these literary tales move simultaneously on many levels and with a visual candor. It is almost as if Mister Bowden split his creative sensibility in moving from boy to man: the verbal bubbles or lettering (as they are called) in the graphic novels split off to become fictions; while the images morphed into fine artworks. They became stand-alone paintings in their own right.

Kratos deals with insanity but on distinct levels, some of which fast forward and back—while parallel dimensions, parts of the mind, stray visual eddies or prisms, and telescoped refractions all recur. This filmic quality proceeds throughout the piece akin to Hitchcock or Blatty, but a strong narrative impulse bestrides this magic realism. It lends the excoriation at the tale's end something akin to the reverberation of Greek tragedy.

From a Right-wing or elitist perspective, I think that Bowden's fictional trajectory works in the following manner. From the very beginning there is an exoteric dimension (much like the political trappings of a reasonably notorious political movement from early in the 20th century). This deals with the artistry, story, structure, prism effect in terms of H. T. Flint's *Physical Optics*, as well as the narratives dealt with above.

But, in my view, there is another hidden, buried, esoteric, occultistic, and numinous aspect. It is slightly and from a liberal perspective rather scandalously linked to a thesis in the book *Nietzsche, Prophet of Nazism* by a Lebanese and Maronite intellectual,[1] together with the occultistic text *The Morning of the Magicians*. This inner urge or poetic trope is an attempt to create the Superman via a manipulation of consciousness.

Most Western cultural standards, menhirs, sacred stones, or objects on the ground have been devastated or destroyed—even though the odd echo can be heard. (This might be said to be a small Classics department at a provincial university, for instance.) Nonetheless, Bowden preaches reintegration—beginning within oneself—and ending up with the maximalization of strength. One should remember or factor in that almost every other literary tendency is contrary or reverse-wise. Characters are chaotic, broken, stunted, uncertain, apolitical, non-religious, without any metaphysic whatsoever, chronically afraid, sexually and emotionally neurotic, tremulous about death, etc.... While Bowden's *oeuvre* intimates the reordination of the Colossus—both gradually and over time.

Hence we begin to perceive a glacial imprimatur in his work; in that characterization is non-Dual, beyond good and

---

[1] Abir Taha, *Nietzsche, Prophet of Nazism: The Cult of the Superman* (Bloomington, Ind.: AuthorHouse, 2006)

evil, semi-gnostic, power-oriented in the manner of Thrasymachus, "demented," furious, even non-Christian. It ennobles the prospect of Odin without the overlay of Marvel Comics and as a Trickster God . . . i.e., it's the moral equivalent of Batman's Joker as reviewed, via *The Dark Knight*, elsewhere on this site.[2] It also ramifies with the words of the anti-humanist intellectual, Bill Hopkins, who, in a cultural magazine close to the polymath Colin Wilson known as *Abraxas*, once remarked: "The purpose of literature is to create New Titans."

One other cultural idea suffices here . . . this has to do with Joseph Goebbels' answer to a question about his interpretation of the Divine. This should be seen as part of the frontispiece of his expressionist novel *Michael*, a third positionist work from the '20s. He described "God" as a multi-proportioned or eight-limbed idol, replete with heavy jambs and rubiate eyes, and possibly constructed from orange sandstone. Such an effigy was associated with the following: flaming tapers or torches, brands, naked female dancers, and human sacrifice. To which the Herr Doktor's interlocutor remarked: "It doesn't sound very Christian to me!" The propaganda minister's response came back as quick as a shot: "You're mistaken; *that is Christ!*"

I think that Jonathan Bowden believes much the same about the meta-ethic of his own literary output. The other stories in this volume were "Origami Bluebeard" (a marriage, a murder, a threnody, a Ragman, a take on Thomas Carlyle's *Sartor Resartus*); "Grimaldi's Leo" (a lighter variant on Animal Liberation), and "Napalm Blonde." This was an attempt at Greek tragedy, configures a Tiresius who may be alone but not in a wasteland, and happens to be radically heterosexualist after Anthony Ludovici's analysis.

For those who have ears to hear—let them hear.

John Michael McCloughlin
Counter-Currents/*North American New Right*
October 9, 2010

---

[2] Trevor Lynch, Review of *The Dark Knight*, Counter-Currents/*North American New Right*, September 27, 2010, http://www.counter-currents.com/2010/09/the-dark-knight/

Jonathan Bowden's *The Fanatical Pursuit of Purity*

Jonathan Bowden
The Fanatical Pursuit of Purity
London: The Spinning Top Club, 2008

This book was published in 2008 by the Spinning Top Club in London. It is a Gothic or picaresque novel of 178 pages. This book can be considered in two basic ways. The first revolves around purely literary considerations. These have to do with an external or diachronic quality which Wyndham Lewis first explicated in the '20s or before.

His aesthetic—very much influenced by his career as a painter—views mankind from the outside. A strategy that is intimately related, in turn, to the portrait painter's desire to get closer and closer to the sitter—almost in a manner which portends a threatening encounter. To wit: in this regard, one remembers Graham Sutherland's portrait of Churchill after the war. It was destroyed by Clementine and the Churchill family—thereby setting back the British taxpayer £80,000 (quite a sizeable amount in the '50s). Churchill hated the painting. He declared grandly: "It makes me look thick—and I ain't!" Always the joker, eh? Nonetheless, the revisionist biography of Churchill by Professor Charmley from Cambridge University features this portrait on the cover.

The point of this digression is that a "Right-wing" view of letters often leads to an exteriorization of Style. This tends to concentrate on a grotesque or Baroque build-up of language which both Lewis and Céline accessed in their fiction. In no matter how crude or dialectical a way (in cultural politics) this was contrasted to the interior monologue or consciousness stream in James Joyce or Virginia Woolf, for example. Perhaps the most gargantuan and gross attempt to do this was Wyndham Lewis' satire, *The Apes of God*. This gigantic tome anatomized English culture in the late '20s with a painter's or an externalist's eye.

Bowden's novel, on the other hand, deals with a retinue of puppets in a marionette show who are marshalled by the late Eric Brammall. (Note: he was a very famous puppeteer from North Wales who wrote extensively about this *folk* art in the British '50s.) Like superheroes in graphic novels, the purity of puppets means that you can be as extreme, heroic, or trans-rational with them as you like. This gives free rein to violent, illiberal fantasy or the need for escape!

An important point was made by the British militant and nationalist Joe Owens in a recent post about a film review on this site[1] . . . he regarded undue immersion in fantasy as negative, counter-propositional, even set up by one's enemies. This is an important point and was well expressed by him. Yet I believe that Bowden would disagree.

Liberal humanist societies—as currently perceived by those who live in them—are incredibly boring. Most citizens, subjects of the Crown (or whatever), seek escape from the above brown fug. Nor is this only marked in adolescence or childhood—although it may be most obvious then. I think that the real point is the nature of the fantasy engaged in and heroic, violent, semi-conscious, militantly engendered (i.e., radically male or female), and elitist material of this sort worries critical establishmentarianism. Hence we see the fact that most Western arts faculties have a methodology (post-structuralism) through which to view it so as to always end up with the "correct" interpretation. War literature—for example—is regarded as qualitatively dangerous in many a Cultural Studies department.

Nonetheless, the use of a heroic puppet called Phosphorous Cool in Bowden's narrative (with legions of minor or supporting characters) in two basic plot lines, leads to variously transgressive outcomes. All of these relate, *en passant*, to Antonin Artaud's Theatre of Cruelty which relates very much to cinema

---

[1] http://www.counter-currents.com/2010/09/inception/ #comment-891

directors like Alfred Hitchcock. For Hitchcock, as Camille Paglia has observed, the real point is to paint on screen with the actors available. This is another exterior vision—one which does little to ameliorate the imagination's authoritarian bias.

The other of the two points about Bowden's fiction, in my opinion, is the anti-dualism of the main antagonists. There are few heroes or villains in his work but combinations of the two instead. If you were to take this Superhuman or Inhumanist notion out of fiction altogether . . . you might end up with some interesting ideas.

Almost everyone grows up with the idea that Wilhelmine Germany (Prussianism and so on) was "bad"; the Allied powers are correspondingly benign. The same idolatry or Aunt Sally tactics are used again and again.

What if these things were more gray, indeterminate, powerful, non-Christian, and Pagan in specificity (à la Nietzsche's *Beyond Good and Evil*)? Isn't it at least a fact, if only provisionally, that if you approached Second World War historicism from a different prism one might understand today's world better? Mightn't the truth lie dynamically between two texts at either end of a metaphoric bookshelf—perhaps Martin Gilbert's Churchill biography and David Irving's *The Mare's Nest*?

If one begins to view the heroic urge in this way then one foregrounds the screenplay writing of John Milius, for instance, but one can also proceed beyond it to Ernst Jünger or Henry de Montherlant. For, if one takes these artistic notions of reprisement on board, then might Bowden be described as doing artistically what certain revisionists are attempting in more factual or non-fictional ways over time. Who knows? Anyway, when Professor George Steiner wrote his play, *The Portage of A. H. to San Cristobal*, over 30 years ago he implicitly recognized that criticism wasn't enough.

For those who have ears to hear—let them hear!

John Michael McCloughlin
Counter-Currents/*North American New Right*
October 3, 2010

JONATHAN BOWDEN'S
A BALLET OF WASPS

Jonathan Bowden
A Ballet of Wasps
London: The Spinning Top Club, 2008

A Ballet of Wasps is a collection of four short stories and a play. The stories (including two that are very short) are "A Ballet of Wasps," "Golgotha's Centurion," "Wilderness' Ape," and "Sixty-Foot Dolls." The play in question is called *Stinging Beetles* and very much relates to the book which follows it in the sequence, *Lilith Before Eve*. The entire volume appeared towards the end of 2008.

Like all of Jonathan Bowden's works, this volume supports radical inequality and the courage which is necessary to view life tragically. The entire point of this corpus of stories is to raise courage and instill qualities of stoicism, anti-defeatism, non-resignation, arrogance, and defeat's absence. One is reminded of the anti-humanist intellectual Bill Hopkins here, who, in writing in the journal *Abraxas* commented that "the purpose of literature is to produce new Titans."

This demarcates Bowden's efforts from a lot of contemporary material—much of which oscillates between entertainment and a reconfirmation of liberal values. There is an important point here—since Bowden's work avoids a great deal of the scatological, vegetative, or crepuscular horror of the area which he has made his own. If one compares his work to the eyeball-removing machine in Edward Bond's *Lear*, for instance, then his fiction is positively genteel.

Nonetheless, in these particular stories, I believe that Bowden is attempting to go beyond mood music in order to impinge upon the reader beneath the conscious mind. Can authors really influence their readers in this way? It remains a moot point. Yet many people act as if there can be uncontrollable impacts (at whatever level) from work they find disagreeable. A large number of conservatives would be made deeply uncomfortable if they had to read through Bertolt Brecht's *The Threepenny Opera* (replete with an Otto Dix painting on the Penguin jacket). Likewise, a fragmentary and volcanic narrative by Louis-Ferdinand Céline would make many a liberal humanist shudder. Imagine quite a few callow PC types having to wade through *Castle to Castle* or *North*—never mind *Guignol's Band* (set in London) or the even more "transgressive" works like *Bagatelles* or Céline's account of his trip to the Soviet Union.

In any event, the very fact of this tremulousness may lead to the idea of deep immersion—particularly in relation to highly imaginative material. I think Bowden's work is an attempt, fictionally speaking, to re-engineer elements of the semi-conscious mind. Hence we see a certain aggression or voltaic energy which is redolent of many "conservative" creators like Belloc, Lewis, or Mencken, but that certainly alienates a conventional or middle-brow perspective.

Similarly, quite a few authors in the Gothic area—one thinks of Lovecraft or Poe—deliberately engage in mesmerism or a phenomenon similar to a séance. This ramps up the level of abstraction, illusion, dream-material, oneiric wonder, or phantasy via more and more baroque language. Yet is this more than dark poetry? Well, it depends upon how you wish to gaze upon it.

Mister Bowden's "religious" ideas are not immediately discernible from his work, but certain items do stand out over time. One is the notion that every type of mysticism exists at this level—even if it doesn't. Another viewpoint suggests that art is the *praxis* of religion. One has the idea with this creator that, *passim*. Goebbels, if asked whether human sacrifice was wrong he would answer: it depends how aesthetically it's done. The British "conceptual" artist Damien Hirst got into very hot water indeed for expatiating on the Twin Towers (September the 11th, 2001) and referring to the aesthetic pleasure they gave him. This is the dandy's position, if you will. Although my own view is that this author attempts to do more.

My suspicion is that he configures his work as a drug, a

transmission mechanism, an occultism, and an estranging mystique. I dispute that he wishes to adopt a mood—rather, in my view, I think that he sees his artistic work as a magical act. This would explain its extreme conservatism—metaphysically speaking—when combined with certain modernist and gruesome aesthetics that many philistines can't stomach. The old conundrum where ideologues who talk much about Western culture are not able to sit through Aeschylus' *Agamemnon* raises its head here.

One is also reminded of the fact that the entire postmodern vista is the '60s creation, and that Timothy Leary's adoption of a drug addict's lifestyle lay at its heart. Narcotics are about many things; overcoming boredom, the tediousness of a liberal society, a desire to escape, personal weakness, etc. Yet, in an artistic sense, I think something crucial is happening here. Bowden as an individual is probably quite puritanical or ascetic, but he believes in the sheer power of the imagination. I believe that if the unsuspecting *voyeur* opens up to what Michael Moorcock once described as fantasy's implicit fascism then Bowden has seized a device with which to hook, deprogram, turn around, and reorient a generation. It must be said that your average liberal academic would regard this as preposterous and meaningless. And yet . . . why insist on an anti-essentialist or "politically correct" method for reading literature in every college if this weren't so?

To finish, "A Ballet of Wasps" concerns a Woodsman's discomfiture about boasting in front of a vampire. It is set in White Russia. "Golgotha's Centurion" is a Sicilian revenge tragedy which owes something to the sweat of John Webster's brow. "Wilderness' Ape" deals with Haitian Voodoo and is quite clearly influenced by Spenser St. John, Revilo P. Oliver, and Lothrop Stoddard in doing so. "Sixty Foot Dolls" explores evolution, degeneration theory, and some of David Icke's more fanciful conundrums. Whilst the play, *Stinging Beetles*, turns around the necessity for courage and involves a dilemma or choice at Life's crossroads. It is less William Styron's exemplification of *Sophie's Choice* than a man's desire to rescue a beautiful blonde girl from a magicians' village. In magical lore, such a hamlet only materializes on a windswept and torrential night.

Perhaps those who believe in the natural goodness of Man

and liberal equity should bear in mind the poem at the volume's start. It exists tucked away on the copyright page.

Study for Three Figures at the Base of a Crucifixion by Francis Bacon (1947):

> Out they stand in orange
> Screaming like blinded bats
> Wrapped around in lintel
> A mother's angel sings:
> *Better were it, indeed, not to be born!*

John Michael McCloughlin
Counter-Currents/*North American New Right*
September 27, 2010

JONATHAN BOWDEN'S
LILITH BEFORE EVE

Jonathan Bowden
Lilith Before Eve
London: The Spinning Top Club, 2009

This book contains four plays which are more likely to be read than played in the theatre. They are called *Lilith Before Eve*, *Glock's Abattoir*, *We Are Wrath's Children!*, and *Evolution X*. This tradition of literary theatre is quite well-known in Britain, but something else needs to be pointed out to make sense of it. This has to do with the "takeover" of the theatrical space in the 1970s and '80s—throughout the British Isles—by the revolutionary Left. A whole raft of authors who were strongly influenced by Brecht and the Berlin Ensemble (in East Germany) gathered the reins of state-subsidized theatre into their hands. They were a veritable hydra whose names included Edward Bond, Arnold Wesker, Howard Brenton, Trevor Griffiths, Jim Allen, Margaret D'Arcy, John Arden, David Edgar, and Caryl Churchill (say).

For example, Brenton describes himself as a "practical communist," Allen was formally linked with the Workers Revolutionary Party (a tiny Marxist-Leninist sect), and Griffiths wrote the screenplay for Warren Beatty's *Reds*. He never joined the Communist Party of Great Britain (CPGB), but actively fellow-traveled.

In many respects, these four plays by Jonathan Bowden are a response to the above, in that they proved to be Right-wing, elitist, non-humanist, inegalitarian, and Nietzschean. A fifth dream play, *Stinging Beetles*, occurred in another volume, *A Ballet of Wasps*, which takes it outside our remit.

Superficially speaking, *Lilith Before Eve* concerns a ventriloquist who loses control of his dummy, *Glock's Abattoir* deals with a caretaker at a cemetery who cries wolf too often, *We Are*

Wrath's Children! involves a battle over a will, and *Evolution X* is an attack on communist brainwashing.

The last play of the four is the most explicitly anti-Leftist, in that it considers the reality which Francis Pollini dealt with in his novel *Night*, published in the early '60s. This text—at once highly demotic and experimental in form—couldn't find an American publisher. A fact which was probably due to its unheroic ethos and its depiction of G.I. degradation, or brainwashing, at the hands of Maoist interrogators.

Bowden's play *Evolution X*, on the other hand, deals with a quiet, isolated, stoic and provincial hermit who is tortured into conformity by Red Guards—or possibly the secret police. He was then turned into a spy behind enemy lines, but survives in order to wreak a terrible revenge. For the spirit of Sophocles' Theban Plays always lurks behind these particular pieces.

Despite their metapolitical intent, all of these works manifest the author's concern with various examples of Anglo-Saxon folk culture. Take, by way of illustration, the Padworth hobby-horse from the English West Country—its dark, Dominican headgear, black coloration, spherical body, tassels, and celebration of a victory over the French, morphs in the United States. It is widely held (by many English cultural historians) to be one of the origins of the trick-or-treating, comedic, and yet slightly "threatening" subculture that fuels the early Ku Klux Klan. This is before the organization re-emerges as an underground army in the South, post defeat, to thwart carpetbagger attempts at Reconstruction. For, in many an English ear, the American accent itself is a radicalization or extension of a Wessex or West Country diction.

In any event, Jonathan Bowden looks at two major forms of English folk art, *in extenso*, during these plays. The first was the Mummers' dramaturgy and the second is Punch and Judy. This playwright quite clearly adores Circus, ventriloquism, music hall, vaudeville, animal taming, Grand Guignol, contortionists, sideshow barkers, mountebanks, Mystery Plays, strong men tearing apart directories, fair grounds, old-fashioned wrestling, ghost trains, escapology, and mesmerism. The Mummers' plays were often without sound, involved blacking-up and Top

Hats, as well as a ubiquitous female figure: the Bessy. They are a very ancient village tradition that often featured sacrifice — by burning like a Guy — at their summation.

Punch and Judy, by contrast, has lasted in one form or another for centuries, but the modern tradition harks back two hundred years to the late 18th century. It is an Italian import which involves glove puppets who are controlled, in the booth, by a manipulator known as the Professor. Punch is a cardinal nightmare or Prince of Folly (possibly the first Tarot card) who beats his wife, throws the baby out of the window, attempts to murder his benign familiar, Clown Joey, and ends up eaten by a Crocodile. This saurian is a synonym for a Dragon who also stands for the Devil. Punch often beats the Devil and jumps up and down on him, in a reverse Gnostic or transgressive touch. Doctor Johnson commented on this extensively in the 18th century. He once snapped, "the first Whig [liberal] was the Devil." One notion which is never commented on, however, is that Punch and Judy is a purely Aryan or Gentile form. No Ashkenazic can be a Professor. The reason being that pork sausages actually have to be handled (traditionally) during the performance, hence all the tomfoolery about porkers involving Punch, Clown Joey, the Crocodile, the Doctor, and the Policeman.

It is quite clear that Jonathan Bowden believes that the antidote to cultural Marxism is folkish (at least in part). This is accompanied by an insight which was borne by the violence of these popular forms. For in modern art — power is beauty.

John Michael McCloughlin
Counter-Currents/*North American New Right*
September 12, 2010

JONATHAN BOWDEN'S
GOODBYE, HOMUNCULUS!

Jonathan Bowden
Goodbye, Homunculus!
London: The Spinning Top Club, 2009

This volume consists of four stories of approximately equal length. Their titles are "Goodbye, Homunculus!," "Iron Breath," "Armageddon's Village," and "Noughts are Crosses." Each one of them deals with extreme takes on the imagination, and the entire book teeters on the edge of various genres. These are Horror, the Gothic, science fiction or romanticism, fantasy, chillers, crime (yes and no), the ghost story, and *noir*. Yet, in all honesty, a serious undertone or classic element lurks throughout, and this has to do with Greek tragedy.

Why has the author composed them? Well, on clear inspection, several discrete pathways or strands become discernible.

The first is a change in moral temperature throughout these tales. At first, this can be rather disconcerting to a half-attentive reader. For it is relatively difficult to tease apart the good from the bad characters. Usually, in tales of this sort, there is a clear distinction. Let's take, for example, the Gothic or *noir* stories of William F. Harvey. Despite his "harm none" or Quakerish views, his astounding or graveyard riffs were "nasty," fierce, clammy, vaguely unwholesome, and ghoulish. The two viewpoints probably went with each other — on reflection. Even Harvey admitted that good attracts evil, so the inner paradox of his compendia becomes clear. He is a classic dualist — irrespective of his literary quality and sepulchral imagination. Essentially Harvey is a Manichean, an either/or man, who posits the notion that God and Satan are coeval.

Bowden, on the other hand, manifests a different approach, since all his varied *personae* seem to be quite clearly a mixture of light and dark, positive and negative, benign or malignant. They wax lyrical as "raptors who feed on blood only to be disappointed," as well as exhibiting the odd tender moment. Most certainly, they are objects or puppets up to a point, and this lends an element of satire to these proceedings. But we have to be careful here: they don't lack reality and even retain a capacity for suffering. For instance, of the two brothers Gregory Fawcett Greensleeve in "Goodbye, Homunculus!" one is quite clearly more Luciferian than the other . . . but the more well-rounded character proves to be multifaceted. Again, in "Iron Breath" both the robot who would replace Mankind—personified by the lonely Lighthouse man—and his "victim" wax *Beyond Good and Evil*. There has to be a medley or interplay of forces. Perhaps, as in Walter Allen's early review of *Tarr* by Wyndham Lewis, humans want to have their cake and eat it.

What does this lead to? Are we in a situation where these stories prove to be transgressive or amoral? That is, do they manifest the architecture of anti-heroes or heroines, as perceived? Such a trajectory would bring them quite close to Aleister Crowley's novels *The Moonchild* and *The Diary of a Drug Fiend*. We might also be treading on Ayn Rand's territory here—if we examine works like *We the Living* (an anti-Soviet piece) or *The Fountainhead*. (Rand is qualitatively different, since her fictional creations live out some libertarian-individualist axioms. But the point still holds.)

Nonetheless, Jonathan Bowden seems to be attempting something quite distinct. To my mind, he is positing a hierarchical or aristocratic morality of high and low. It involves the substitution of one system of ethics (Judeo-Christian) with another (Byronic, Classical, Pagan, or power-moral). Yet it is not a replacement of the better by the worse. Nor can we exempt from our schema the fact that liberal humanism can be considered as secularized Christianity.

Does this mean that he is advocating anti-ethics as traditionally perceived? No, not really . . . for such varied systems preach dog-eat-dog, to the victor the spoils, morality amounts to little more than the laughter of the strongest man, etc. Such nostrums can be associated with Hobbes' social theories, the black opal-like philosophies of the Marquis de Sade, or Antinomianism.

(The last comes across as either heresy or a dissenting note within Calvinism. It derived from alternative ideas about predestination and election inside Puritanism as a whole. Many of these views subtly influenced various subcultures in the early United States. By far the clearest explication of them is in James Hogg's classic of Scotch literature, *The Confessions of a Justified Sinner*. A text that André Gide, a self-confessed existential or immoralist, revived in the early 20th century.)

To recap: I don't believe that Bowden is advocating moral inversion, "Satanism," or pseudo-Satanism at all. No, he happens to be promoting aristocratic radicalism and its attendant *mores*. Put more earnestly, it amounts to the ethical attitudes of the Vikings or Odinists. This means that infighting (even within an individual) is moral, honor proves to be the linchpin of behavior, and that everything ramifies with Nature. Each and every person has his natural place within a hierarchy, biology overmasters life, striving is moral, strength welcomes morality, and the weak should be punished—but they can become stronger. This is by virtue of the fact that all valuable forms of life open out and grow towards the sun. By dint of this lexicon, immorality—theft, lying, drug addiction, false manipulation of others, perversion—stands out as weak and *vice versa*. Such a prognosis occurs most nakedly in "Noughts Are Crosses"—a critique of materialism at one level, and the third story, "Armageddon's Village."

In "Armageddon's Village," the paraplegic husband and recluse, Spider Absinthe Marmaduke, may be helpless in relation to the brewing conspiracy against his life. Yet he is determined to enact the prospect of vengeance—even beforehand. So it proves to be the intensity of his gaze (his desire to live) which puts off his assailant long enough to lead to a cataclysmic *deus ex machina*.

These are pagan tales *tout court*: in them justice is revenge. Needless to say, even the disabled or afflicted can be eugenic if they crawl towards the sun with a knife between their teeth.

And at the end . . . everything goes back into Nature so as to start over.

John Michael McCloughlin
Counter-Currents/*North American New Right*
September 3, 2010

Jonathan Bowden's *Louisiana Half-Face*

Jonathan Bowden
Louisiana Half-Face
London: The Spinning Top Club, 2010

Louisiana Half-Face was published in the first half of 2010. It continues a projected literary cycle which began with *The Fanatical Pursuit of Purity*—at least thematically. This novel fits into the horror genre most explicitly and draws on various icons from this set. These include Mummies, Skeleton-Men (the figure of Dramabu in Haitian Voodoo), a da[e]mon called Cranium Biter Dye, and a split-face or schizoid character which gives the book its title. But this has less to do with a Right-wing version of Burroughs than one might suspect.

My estimation is that Bowden configures contemporary horror writing to be de-intellectualized tragedy. If, for example, Stephen King, Anne Rice, or Graham Masterton began to philosophize about motivation then they would lose about 80% of their audience without comment. Indeed, as a literary sideline, the crudity of current Gothic prose signals its "proletarianization"—to use an image from the conservative essayist Professor Duncan Williams in *Trousered Apes*. Just on a literary level: there is little comparison between Algernon Blackwood, Arthur Machen, Walter de la Mare, and contemporary purveyors of "slasher" items or gore.

Yet this remains a sideline to the author's main concerns. Much of contemporary artistic life (although very interesting) is without any reliable meaning. A genuine semi-nihilism—of a Bret Easton Ellis type—hangs over Western culture like a pall. How did the Ancients and the restorationists of early Modernity, the Renaissance, impute an engagement with life . . . with Heidegger's Being? Well, it was primarily through a tragic or ennobling sense of life. If one computes tragedy as literary horror, underpinned by philosophical acuity, then you begin to realize that this author believes in reintegration.

One of the reasons he concentrates on slightly cruder or "lower" forms, like horror, is their presence beneath the literary radar. No ideas or concepts of culture are ever destroyed—they are merely displaced. Where did the belletrism of identity and the heroic—even a threnody of the cruel or violent—really go? The answer is that it went down into mass culture—essentially despised by the New Criticism (F. R. Leavis and I. A. Richards) of the mid-20th century.

Even more acutely: where did fascistic literature of an ultra-masculine cast go? Why, at the level of Wyndham Lewis' *The Apes of God*, Henry de Montherlant's *The Bachelors*, and Yukio Mishima's *Sea of Fertility*, did it disappear altogether? But many of these themes, stripped of poetry and intellect, re-emerge as actions in mass culture. The extreme Left, as exemplified by the post-structuralist school, is deeply aware of this conundrum as well as the dangerous "essentialisms" lurking down there in the depths.

One interesting sidelight on contemporary travails is seen by the fate of Professor Paul de Man at Yale University. He headed the school of deconstruction there. This is the detailed, linguistic and hermeneutical examination of mass culture. Amongst its ideological beliefs are the ideas that authors have nothing to do with their texts, empirical facts in historical writing (for example) have no validity, and everything is relative. Well, it turned out that Professor de Man had fellow-traveled with the Rexist movement in Belgium during the Second World War. He had also contributed mildly nationalist articles to a review like Michael Walker's *The Scorpion*, for instance. (For those not in the know, Operation Skorpion was the Europeanization of the Waffen SS's ideology—as Alan Clark revealed in his history *Barbarossa*.) Nonetheless, de Man's crime was such that the late post-structural or deconstructive school has been fatally crippled by this brief flirtation with the other. By which I mean those forces in the European subconscious which a present-day English literati called Ian McEwan describe as the "black dogs."

I leave it to your imagination what tendency of opinion these wolves represent. Yet, suffice it to say, that in the cast list of James Herbert's *The Spear* (based on Trevor Ravenscroft's *The Spear of Destiny*) the extreme Right is the villain. One could argue—from this perspective—that this trail is exemplified perfectly by Ira Levin's *The Boys from Brazil* (for example).

Yet if radical elitism, in its customary guise, is always the enemy . . . then what about an example of horror fiction which also contains a strong dose of European cultural fundamentalism? Surely that would be the worst thing in the world—in a doubled up or *Inglourious Basterds* sort of way. What could be more "Situationist," more transgressive, than "Right wing" horror . . . at least on another level of reality?

On a rival plane altogether, the New Left Marxist Theodor Adorno, in a text called *Minima Moralia*, said that all poetry was redundant after Auschwitz-Birkenau. Everything! Well, imagine if even that implacable and postmodern logic was contradicted by the tragic idolatry of a form which worships a Nature that is neither good nor bad. What begins with the sinister Baroque of H. P. Lovecraft can become over time the attitudinizing of Savitri Devi—albeit filtered through multiple levels of estrangement, denial, advance, and projected awe.

Interestingly, this volume is dedicated to Savitri Devi with a brief poem on the copyright recto—a page in most books which is customarily ignored by readers. It befits a *daughter of the black sun*, as its anonymous bard describes it.

"John Michael McCloughlin"
Counter-Currents/*North American New Right*
September 19, 2010

About the Author

JONATHAN BOWDEN, April 12, 1962–March 29, 2012, was a British novelist, playwright, essayist, painter, actor, and orator, and a leading thinker and spokesman of the British New Right.

Born in Kent and largely self-educated, Bowden was involved with a series of Right-wing groups for which he was a popular speaker, including the Monday Club, the Western Goals Institute, the Revolutionary Conservative Caucus, the Freedom Party, the Bloomsbury Forum, the British National Party, and finally the New Right (London), of which he was the Chairman.

Bowden was a prolific author of fiction, philosophy, criticism, and commentary. His books include *Mad* (1989), *Aryan* (1990), *Sade* (Egotist, 1992), *Brute* (Egotist, 1992), *Skin* (Egotist, 1992), *Axe* (Egotist, n.d.), *Craze* (Egotist, 1993), *Right* (European Books Society, 1993), *Collected Works* (Avant-garde, 1995), *Standardbearers: British Roots of the New Right*, edited with Adrian Davies and Eddy Butler (Beckenham, Kent: The Bloomsbury Forum, 1999), *Apocalypse TV* (London: The Spinning Top Club, 2007), *The Fanatical Pursuit of Purity* (London: The Spinning Top Club, 2008), *Al-Qa'eda MOTH* (London: The Spinning Top Club, 2008), *Kratos* (London: The Spinning Top Club, 2008), *A Ballet of Wasps* (London: The Spinning Top Club, 2008), *Goodbye Homunculus!* (London: The Spinning Top Club, 2009), *Lilith Before Eve* (London: The Spinning Top Club, 2009), *Louisiana Half-Face* (London: The Spinning Top Club, 2010), *Colonel Sodom Goes to Gomorrah* (London: The Spinning Top Club, 2011), *Our Name is Legion* (London: The Spinning Top Club, 2011), *Locusts Devour a Carcass* (London: The Spinning Top Club, 2012), and *Spiders are Not Insects* (London: The Spinning Top Club, 2012).

Bowden's paintings, drawings, and cartoons can be seen in *The Art of Jonathan Bowden (1974–2007)* (London: The Spinning Top Club, 2007), *The Art of Jonathan Bowden, Vol. 2 (1968–1974)* (London: The Spinning Top Club, 2009), and *The Art of Jonathan Bowden, Vol. 3 (1967–1974)* (London: The Spinning Top Club, 2010).